Copyright ©2015

ISBN 9780692443965
LCCN2014907092

All rights reserved. No part of this book may be reproduced or transmitted in any form or by any means, electronic or mechanical, including photocopying, recording, or by any information storage and retrieval system, without permission in writing from the copyright owner.

This book was printed in the United States of America.
To order additional copies contact the Publisher:

Email: Hollismediagroup@outlook.com
Website: www.Hollismedia.net

"CHURCH GIRLS" the Seduction of Religion

I cannot glamorize how I lived, it happened. In retrospect, I wish my path would have been different and my mind more stabled at the time to avoid the dark vortex that ensued after attending a church service. However, through God's grace, my soul was finally pulled out of the abyss of sexual enslavement. An entrapment not wished upon anyone — that sphere is filled with grand delusion where one thinks he or she is serving God but is grossly deceived by lust.

ALTHOUGH events in your life can render you torn and afflicted but don't lose hope, the supremacy of GOD can make things brand new if you will not capitulate and give you courage to begin again. My desire is for my change to heal someone else's pain–

Sincerely,
"A Church Girl"...

I Timothy 4: 1, 4 &5

1Now the Spirit speaks expressly, that in the latter times some shall depart from the faith, giving heed to seducing spirits, and doctrines of devils.

4For every creature of God is good, and nothing to be refused, if it be received with thanksgiving: 5For it is sanctified by the word of God and prayer.

Quote from Dr. Martin Luther King
Breaking the Silence April 4, 1967

Dr. King wrote this regarding the "Vietnam War" however, the moral of the lesson is so appropriate to address the abuse of power in religious settings.

"Some of us who have already begun to break the silence of the night have found that the calling to speak is often a vocation of agony, but we must speak. We must speak with all the humility that is appropriate to our limited vision, but we must speak. And we must rejoice as well, for surely this is the first time in our nation's history that a significant number of its religious leaders have chosen to move beyond the prophesying of smooth patriotism to the high grounds of a firm dissent based upon the mandates of conscience and the reading of history. Perhaps a new spirit is rising among us. If it is, let us trace its movement well and pray that our own inner being may be sensitive to its guidance, for we are deeply in need of a new way beyond the darkness that seems so close around us."

"CHURCH GIRLS" the Seduction of Religion

TABLE OF CONTENT

DEDICATION		7
PRELUDE		8
Chapter 1	No Ordinary Day	12
Chapter 2	Granny in the Mix	20
Chapter 3	Dark Culture	24
Chapter 4	Destined to Serve	32
Chapter 5	I Was Hooked	42
Chapter 6	From Sinner to Sinful	53
Chapter 7	Jezebel	59
Chapter 8	The Beginning of the End	80
Chapter 9	Church Convention	89
Chapter 10	Can I Be Redeemed?	109
Chapter 11	Is It Finally Over?	123
Chapter 12	No Turning Back	143
Chapter 13	The Telephone Call	160
Chapter 14	I Will Be Your Angel	168
Chapter 15	No More Demons	175
Chapter 16	Making a Choice	178
Chapter 17	Finally Over	190

Appendix A- A Church Girl Demonized	193
Personality Summary Dr. McKenzie -	197
The Parallel Composition	201
Resource Index	203
About the Authors	205

DEDICATION

This exposé deserves a place at the table and is worthy of dialogue in the global community of faith, and when warranted, to be processed in the corridors of justice.

It is undeniably a privilege to be in position to inspire development of another's life—to encourage global exploration, to strengthen one's personal commitment that increases appreciation of our individuality and to remind of our obligation to give back to the "Collective." For we are our brother's keeper. Therefore, this true story was published to empower those without *voice* to find your will to thrive... to demand change for yourself and never allow anyone to silence your purpose because ALL life is valuable.

May Almighty GOD restore, renew and release to you a long awaited new beginning.

PRELUDE

Without question sex trafficking is big business! In addition, one would not automatically equate sex trafficking and religion in the same sentence. However, what most will struggle to understand is how many young females succumb to being exchanged (swapped) within networks among ministers. Of course, these so-called holy men are stoic and view it as an entitlement whilst some females never recover emotionally from the illicit give-and-take. It is common practice among some sexually addicted clergy to share women with their friends and unfortunately, many church officials continue to gloss over this irreverent behavior without consequences. After all to them 'men will be men.' But the hypocrisy is at full scale because it is those same church officials and clergy that condemn to death homosexuals yet, their personal engagement in illicit trysts are polished and presented as a rite-of-passage.

In addition, it should be a shared concern when we consistently give power to predators both male and female in the name of God; we *entrust* our families seemingly without question to their care and when we remain silent regarding deviant behavior, we too, are conspirators.

The sordid "*Vixen*" spikes one dichotomy of this story. She takes pleasure in sleeping with preachers and thinks nothing of it; to her, the preacher is like any other man, and is unashamedly committed to their destruction while serving in various positions in the church at the pastor's direction. Of course, you've seen her; the 'Vixen' is sometimes the Youth leader, Choir Director, Sunday school teacher, Usher, Choir member, president of the Pastor's Aide and some are so brazen and serve as the president of the Pastor's Wife Aide. Got you thinking? Surely, you have seen her and perhaps could never figure out why she was so contrary to others – the "Vixen" is led to believe that she is the pastor's favorite and is above the rest. Is always opinionated and visually opposes the pastor's wife… and anybody else. She amuses herself with delusions of grandeur and exclusivity, and doesn't realize she is just a NUMBER. In addition, the tide will shift (another woman will take her place) and in the end will lose . . .

The behavior of this type of woman is akin to the biblical reference of a temple prostitute (a.k.a. A modern-day "Church Groupie"); and the sociopath professing to be God's man doesn't discourage the behavior and even coerce some women to perceive sexual service as a sacred one.

Then there are the "Victims": women who are violated sexually and emotionally, and no one seems to care.

What we have is "CHIHIRO." A thousand unanswered questions…

Indisputably, details of the parasitic behavior and irreverent disposition of both laity and leadership reveals an unspoken dark culture in the church, and unfortunately, entangled in this abyss are the husbands; they are cast aside and replaced emotionally and sometimes sexually, by the pastor. Especially in congregations where male pastors offer little or no educational substance; these men rely upon their *sexual prowess* to allure and captivate dissatisfied wives who soak up the attention lavished upon them that isn't given at home.

These predators (male and female), espouse guilt-ridden *subtexts that are designed to control* congregants to submit to their personal demands that are always rooted in greed, and fueled by sociopathic tendencies. However, little do they realize *justice* is already standing at the door.

Just as history has already judged the Catholic Church exposing the atrocious behavior of priests, one must raise the question what about the other churches. Are others more consecrated to GOD as the reason for them being unscathed in these types of scandals? I think not.

Why are Caucasian males seemingly the predominate ones linked to sexual abuse in the church? Without question, there are high rates of unreported sexual abuse among clergy; seemingly, the taboo of not airing your dirty laundry is widely more accepted in some, not all, black and Latina communities.

Notwithstanding, we must continue asking questions, first, is there a cover up? Second, by whom and why?

This philosophical overview is critical; there is tremendous unchecked abuse in some churches among black ministers as well as in certain Latina communities, and unfortunately, the silence is deafening! The rapid criticism by many religious folks is why talk about this; why disparage black preachers? Nothing could be more false; the book recounts a true story — and what's true is "we" should position ourselves to be conduits of healing, inspiration and anything else that represent goodness, but sometimes we are not. Many church people have committed some of the most dastardly acts against one another, and anyone with a long history of being in church knows this is true. Moreover, either some that criticize

"CHURCH GIRLS" the Seduction of Religion

the hardest are involved, know of someone, or wish they could be.

In the White community, Caucasian clergymen are unsparingly strutted before millions in the court of public opinion; Black men of the cloth aren't any different from their white counterparts. But, there appears to be a cover up by those who sit under their leadership…Why? When avoiding the obvious isn't conducive to the church, the community and doesn't represent GOD.

So one question out of tens of thousands is what about the women (the driving economic hand in the black church – in all churches) … what motivates many to stay in abusive clergy surroundings?

Hypocrisy is the *rope* by which many religious figures hang themselves because they suppress women from ascending, but think nothing of coercing or seducing her into sexual slavery… in the name of religion. Yet, the church is SILENT!

"What goes on in some black churches make the Catholic Church look mild; that avalanche is yet to happen, but it will and so many will lose." Said Rev. James of Chicago.

CHAPTER 1

No ordinary day - The Introduction

"CHURCH GIRLS" the Seduction of Religion

As I sat in my office gathering paperwork for a client who was scheduled to arrive, I never imagined a business conversation would lead to a heart wrenching confession of abuse; including sexual enslavement to a renowned pastor and bishop. This sparked the genesis two years later for "Church Girls: the seduction of religion."

Most people think that women who are easily deceived in such situations are weak-minded and unaccomplished; or they think of the unsophisticated, unlearned young girl who has no way out, so she succumbs. Not so.

When my client arrived, it was business as usual to gather information about the project, talk a little about her expectations and provide a scope of what we would do for the project.

Eventually, my client asked me if I knew of a particular bishop. I heard of his name in several settings and slightly knew of his media presence. Well, nothing about the preparation of my morning equipped me for what she said next.

"I was his WHORE!"

I was flabbergasted that this well-educated woman had just compartmentalized her life to that of a whore. That was a first. She didn't flinch when she saw how surprised I was; suddenly I recognized there was more to this than just some woman bragging about her life.

"I made him!" she said. "I taught him how to position himself with certain personalities, to attend the right meetings and made sure he met the right people. Then, after I got him to a place where folks all across the country were calling him, this bastard began acting as if I did not matter. I found out he had other women too."

I didn't know whether to cry for her or try to comfort her. The atmosphere was filled with pain, and disappointment permeated the room. Nevertheless, my client remained very professional. I was unsure where this path would lead, so I just listened.

As her story poured forth, I felt strongly that the woman who sat before me was the prototype of the face of thousands of women who were hurting in silence. Here was a woman clearly connected to GOD and the church—a "Church Girl" who loved a man, who loved no one but himself, not even the wife he already had (*that he lied about*) when the affair began. This is an all too familiar story in religion. The pastor or minister becomes notable (or maybe not), but all too often there is a woman attached to an *illegitimate* relationship somewhere. Even though my client laughed a lot during our visit, it was clear that she was hurting. Nevertheless, she was resolved to use her life experience to help others.

It would be almost two years later before she and I reconnected on this subject. In the meantime, I began to understand more how much pressure is associated with doing business with some male ministers (so many are simply untruthful). Many of them never had any recognition outside of the institution where they currently *preside* or previously served, but for some ungodly and stupid reason some often act as if the world begins and ends with them.

"CHURCH GIRLS" the Seduction of Religion

There were always church stories about ministers and women in the congregation and the confusion that it led to, often resulting in people leaving their church home because of the preacher's sexual indiscretions. We know this is not a shocking revelation. Yet, this story reveals a dark culture rarely addressed — *strippers at church conventions.*

It was common practice for perverted preachers who are afraid to grow old and broke, to always seek out the older women in the church and give them that special attention to guarantee tithes are paid; their offering exceeded the other church members' *commitment*, and they would prepare food and happily serve these preachers without any fuss. On the other hand, within this select group of *sociopathic* ministers, many would travel with a younger member of the congregation for the excitement of feeling younger, wanted and needed. This boosted their ego and *self-esteem*.

However, what I always pushed back against was the willingness of some churchwomen to give the male leader a pass for consistent indiscretions, while at the same time they would gash a woman's character a part without blinking an eye. I could never understand how quickly the religious compassion diminished when it came to helping a young woman that was caught in an embarrassing situation (she didn't sin by herself). Many have fallen so deeply and never recovered because other women in the church kept reminding them of their downfall, whereas they took a position of forgiveness and compassion with the male leader.

Do we even care as women, as Christians, that some women (perhaps older women now) lost their way because they fell in love with a married, religious leader and just lost it? Yet the man's life went on as though nothing ever happened because he still had support from the "sisters." The same "sisters" that blocked the restoration of the female transgressor; "sisters" that gossiped and snickered behind her back, treated her as trash but only had glowing remarks about the male offender, which demonstrates a grave disconnect as would-be Christians.

This book illuminates numerous encounters of a journey and fallacies that promoted destructive behavior, as well as amplified patterns of emotional and psychological abuse in the church that remains uncorrected. Which is criminal.

As a woman, and a minister, I know this story will empower many women to find strength and *their* voice to begin again. And to you I say, "There is so much more to life than what you have experienced." However, let us not misconstrue the intent for encouragement; we are not excusing or condemning, we are keeping it real because with some church folks the hypocrisy is extremely funky. Amazingly, some of the identical *churchwomen* that block other women from moving forward will readily stand by the whore-mongering men, and faithfully give their money. Are we "collectively" such hypocrites (*is it in our DNA ladies*) that we will continue as usual to look the other way as we give good "ol' rev" another pass?

Specifically, looking at this pattern in some churches I know many adopt the mantra of primarily praying for the male pastor; although noble but it is not enough. When a pastor is deviant and demeaning it cannot be over looked just because he is a preacher, and should not especially because he is a "**preacher**."

"CHURCH GIRLS" the Seduction of Religion

Church folks let's get real, sexual addiction is a sickness, and it would demonstrate genuine love to position your pastor for a real chance to get help in lieu of hiding the problem; it doesn't mystically go away. If the pastors are held accountable, knowing that if, a young girl is inappropriately touched or any woman without her consent, then the possibility of incarceration might serve as a deterrent.

In reality, some male pastors can be the biggest pimps and cons, and some "church" women will accept him with open arms without confirming his qualifications to lead them just because he is a man—often accepting his ability to contextually interject scripture in his dialogue as a sign of God's acceptance; and is just plain stupid….

Abuse is abuse, no matter what form. So why do some women stay in these types of churches? Is the treatment from the perpetrator parallel to that of loving a man who do not love you? Many women stay with men who knowingly cheat, sometimes in plain view, who beat and steal from them, in spite of there not being the presence of one's life or that of children in peril.

It is time to introduce an intentional, purposeful dialogue regarding this contaminated culture and condition in the house of worship between the leader, vixen and victim. We all limp on fractured faith, suffer broken hearts, have dashed dreams and need a place to heal without compounded distractions from spiritual leaders who aren't true to GOD.

I scoured the internet looking for stories of reported cases of clergy abuse in the black church during my research and came across this story written in 2013. By the way, we were scolded for even mentioning black preachers being associated with sexual misconduct, which further accentuates the problem in some black communities…you can't enshrine bullshit. You have to flush it.

Monday, January 21, 2013. Commentaries **Clergy sex abuse and "the silence of the many."** The unmistakable message of silence and do-nothingness is that, among Baptists, clergy sex abuse is typically treated as "no big deal."

"True evil lies not in the depraved act of the one, but in the silence of the many." On this day, I am contemplating these words, attributed to a black Baptist preacher, Martin Luther King Jr.

In countless stories of Baptist, clergy sex abuse, we have seen the sad truth of King's words made manifest. Even with childhood histories of horrific abuse — of having been molested, raped and sodomized by Baptist preachers — many have said that the worst of their experience came when they tried to tell about the abuse within the faith community.

That was when they faced "the silence of the many."

That was when the relational fabric of community, and often even of family, was torn asunder.

That was when faith itself was deemed a fraud.

Church after church has stood, not in solidarity with those who have been abused by clergy, but rather, with the accused minister-molesters. Often, the churches have stood with the ministers even when they admit their soul-murdering deeds, and sometimes even when they have been criminally convicted.

Church officials have quietly allowed accused preacher-predators—even those with multiple accusations—"to hop to new churches, and to do so repeatedly."

In the Church of God in Christ denomination at one of its national conventions that used to take place in Memphis, it is a known fact that concubines and mistresses have acted out during services. One female purportedly placed a baby at the base of the pulpit where a bishop was sitting, and walked back to her seat demonstrating her defiance as a result of being cast aside by the bishop. Yet, many officials saw it, and did nothing.

"Parishioners are told that they must take their allegations to the church of the accused minister. This is like telling bloody sheep that, if they want help, they must go to the den of the wolf that savaged them. This system does not work."

The seduction, abuse and disillusionment continues.

CHAPTER 2

GRANNY IN THE MIX...

"CHURCH GIRLS" the Seduction of Religion

It was a sunny weekend, the afternoon my neighbor, who was also one of the church mothers (meaning an elderly woman of distinction or so held in the black church), asked me to come over. I thought it would be the same small talk, including her disgust with her relationship with her husband, Thomas, who had been impotent for seventeen years. She would occasionally remind him during their many arguments if she was losing, "Yeah, Church Mom got *kahunas*."

While we sat sipping tea at the small kitchen table, the conversation shifted to a prominent businessperson and preacher who visited our church twice each year. It was apparent that this elderly woman had taken time to assess that this man had a fondness for me. Her prying eyes baffled me as she continued to talk. In this prominent Baptist church with over 2,000 members, she managed to zero in on this. There is no way this was coincidental; to me, she was alluding that I entertain the preacher, and if he wanted or needed a place to relax away from the congregants that I should bring him to her home where she had an extra bedroom. Mother Thomas wanted to make extra money on the side and this was one way to ensure she would get it if I entertained the guest preacher (Only a Madam operates like this) in her home.

Mother Thomas said unapologetically, "Sis, that man is a nice man and he likes you. I want you to hear me, just listen," she said noticing how uncomfortable I became with the conversation. "He is going to ask you something and don't you tell him no." I smiled, but inwardly thought how awkward and uncomfortable this was because what I was hearing came from a woman old enough to be my great grandmother.

"What do you mean Sister Thomas?" I asked.

She replied, "He likes you."

"How do you know?"

"I can tell," She said. "Now, Sis, if he asks you to go to dinner, go. Don't tell him no."

Of course, later I found out through our extended conversations, that she was suggesting to when the moment came, and it would, if I was approached sexually, I was not to turn him away.

Whew! This was a little heavy coming from a seventy-year-old church mother. She said to me on several occasions, "I look at you like my granddaughter." I thought, what kind of grandmother would tell her granddaughter to have sex with older men? Didn't say it, but I thought it. Mother Thomas would sometimes complain about her elderly friend Mrs. Jamison for being so sex-driven; oh great, another horny old churchwoman I have to hear about. Who in the hell wants to hear this stuff?

I thought being around churchwomen would be so different and enrich my life, but what I learnt was that women in the church connected with visiting clergy as they would with a man in a nightclub. I also became aware that some churchwomen are more dedicated to coming to church to hear guest preachers, than attending church on scheduled worship days. I found this very confusing.

In previous churches I attended, I did not have much direct interaction with any person in a high leadership capacity, so I wasn't sure what to make of Mother Thomas' perspective. Looking back, I can see how what she said helped to set me up for what came next.

    Well, sure enough, the guest preacher did approach me. Thank God, it ended before it got out of hand. This church business is like a circus; filled with all kinds of funny animals.

CHAPTER 3

THE DARK CULTURE CONTINUES

"CHURCH GIRLS" the Seduction of Religion

On a simmering Saturday afternoon, I decided to visit the mall, feeling the need to interact with people instead of sitting in the house watching television the entire day. I had no idea of the surprise that awaited me at the mall.

I was walking through the mall and suddenly noticed this very tall, handsome, well-dressed individual walking towards me from the opposite end of the mall entrance. I knew he was going to speak since he never took his eyes off me; as our path intersected, we both said hello and he quickly asked if he could talk to me for a moment. So I stopped. We exchanged small talk for about ten minutes. Then he abruptly kissed me on the cheek while I was still talking. Who does this to strangers? Later in our conversation, he disclosed he was a pastor and placed a business card in my hand.

"Why don't you come to my church office and talk to me some time when you have a moment?" he suggested.

I have never had a habit of interacting with pastors (I did not want them in my business and intended to keep it this way). Recognizing how hesitant I was, he said again, "Oh come on, you can give me five minutes," he said. "You might find your next church home. Don't knock it until you have a chance to see what we offer."

I felt cornered and was upset with myself for telling him that I didn't attend church. I told him I would think about it, and then found myself saying that I would call.

I waited a few days to call to make an appointment. It was obvious he was accustomed to inviting people to his office because he freely extended the invitation to me.

I thought *what do I know; I am not a pastor, and perhaps this is the way things are done.*

Upon my arrival at his office, a very unpleasant secretary greeted me. She was an older fat woman who looked down over her glasses to size me up, making me very uncomfortable. The way she treated me one would think I was intruding and had done something wrong just for showing up.

When the pastor finally came to the visitor's area to greet me he said, "I am really surprised to see you; I did not think you were going to show up."

"Well pastor, I said I would come."

Surprisingly, he had legitimate questions. He asked me about my previous church home, family life and other things along those lines. Noticing the time because I honestly believed he meant the session would be brief, but no more than fifteen minutes, I picked up my handbag to leave. So I said, "Pastor, thank you, it was nice to learn about what your church has to offer but I haven't made any decision about joining a church."

"Well take your time, it wasn't expected of you to make a decision today — come back to visit us, you never know you might like it here."

As I extended my hand to shake his, he grabbed me and hugged me. As I began pulling away, he took his hand and forced my face to his, and kissed me on the lips; he tried to put his tongue in my mouth. Then he placed one hand on my breast. As I struggled to push him away, he forced my hand on his penis by holding my hand with a death grip; he guided my hand to trace his erection, while holding back the other arm with considerable pressure to ensure I did not move away. I continued to struggle and it was clear to him that I wasn't okay with what he was doing.

Finally, he released me. "Listen, I am really sorry. Are you okay?" he asked, visibly concerned and not knowing what I was going to do about what just happened.

With teary eyes and a big lump in my throat I asked, "Why did you do that?" His behavior was demeaning and perhaps some women would find his actions exciting; at best, it was cheap, and not appreciated. He was an old fart.

"I am so sorry; I did not mean to offend you. I don't know what came over me." And then requested, "Will you call me?"
"No." I said.
"Why not? I just want to talk to you. Don't let what happened today keep you from gaining a friend," he said.

I thought to myself if friendships are made this way why are some men in jail for attempted rape and sexual assault. What a mistake I made going to his office. This incident made me realize that I had allowed myself to venture into unknown territory, and that I should have been more cautious when he exhibited questionable behavior upon our first meeting. At the time, I was going through a troubled period. My husband of thirteen years was pressuring me for a divorce and my self-esteem was at an all-time low. Any spiritual guidance would have served to help me seek for something more in life.

This man just happened to be the first pastor ever to approach me. Although I have never had an encounter like this with another pastor, and it was a huge mistake for not recognizing what this man was. He was a predator with a cunning disposition; it was obvious his behavior was well concealed when it came to women. After some time, I learned he was married with four children.

Then several months later as I began to explore the church scene, I would learn that the women in his church loved him no matter what. Regardless whom I spoke with, if his name was mentioned and the individual was female, they loved him unconditionally. Sometime after this incident, one of my dearest girlfriends, Shannon, called to invite me to her church and not thinking too much about it, accepted the invitation.

"I'll come by and pick you up; you will love it there. My pastor is really wonderful; the music is great, and the atmosphere is so powerful." My friend Shannon was really into this religious stuff. Only God knows what she meant about the atmosphere is 'powerful.'

On the morning she came to pick me up for service, I felt good inside for making an effort to get closer to God by attending church. However, I could not believe my eyes as she turned into the parking lot of the church where I fought off this crazy lustful pastor. I regretted accepting her invitation and wanted to leave, but realized my angst was unfounded since my girlfriend did not know about the encounter. There was no need to make waves with her about her pastor. In addition, since I did not ever have to visit again, convinced myself to sit through the service and be done with the entire experience.

"CHURCH GIRLS" the Seduction of Religion

I was too naive to see that my friend, Shannon, had a crush on her pastor (which she later confessed). She was so enraptured and of course, he was a saint in her eyes. It was "my pastor this, and my pastor that." Often times she would call me to complain about her husband and make comparisons between the two. One Saturday she called me after a very intense argument with her husband, and as she has done on so many occasions cried and lamented about not being loved and appreciated. We talked as usual, but then she started talking about her pastor, and my heart cringed.

"I wish my husband could be like my pastor. He is so sweet and he always compliments his wife. My husband never says anything nice to me except when we are about to have sex."

I chuckled.

"What; why are you laughing?"

"Sorry Shannon, you are crazy."

"I am serious. My husband never has a kind word to say and doesn't appreciate me at all. I really believe he hates women."

"Why do you say that, girl?"

"He is abusive; he cusses me out in public and doesn't show any respect whatsoever. All I am saying is why couldn't God have given me a husband like pastor."

Biting my lip as much as I could, then said, "You don't know what you are saying. How do you know what type of man your pastor is to his wife? He isn't who you think he is...

he isn't!"

I thought she would pull back a little or change the subject altogether, but Shannon was full throttle singing the praises of that darn pervert.

Finally, I said, "The man you see is really a cheater; he is lustful, he groped me the first time I visited his office and forcibly kissed and touched me. Do you want a husband that is a whoremonger who stands behind a lectern and espouses scripture, but doesn't try to live close to anything he teaches?"

There was prolonged silence between us for some time and I thought she hung up on me.

"Shannon. Shannon," I said the second time.
"I'm here," she said.
"How did this happen?" she asked. Then, proceeded to question the validity of my story with several more questions stating it was hard to fathom this happening. In essence, she called me a liar.

I really did not care although it wasn't long before she cunningly let me know how she felt.

A month or so had passed and we were casually talking on the phone when her favorite *pastime* came up (meaning her pastor—the black god of her universe).

"I thought about what you said my pastor did and I find it hard to see him acting this way, why would he? She said. What is so special about *you* that he would need to ask *you* for anything?" She asked in a mean-spirited condescending tone.

I had to process did Shannon just ask me what is so special about me; in my heart I felt like cussing her out but what would that achieve. This was demeaning to me.

However, I realized the "black god" to many lonely hurting black women like Shannon is always protected no matter what, even when the evidence is staring them in the face. Notwithstanding, White women have equally as much attachment to their spiritual leaders and a few have murdered the competition in the name of love.

It cannot be God-related as to why some black women are in denial about the men they call pastor. Why pastors are excused without any accountability does not compute. Not only women, but also some men idolized Shannon's pastor as well. The way his parishioners spoke about him one would think he was a black god.

It seemed so. Eventually, I became one of those women.

CHAPTER 4

DESTINED TO SERVE

"CHURCH GIRLS" the Seduction of Religion

It was the summer of 1993 when I first met "the preacher."

Earlier that year, my husband had asked for a divorce because he had decided that he was in love with the secretary, the housekeeper, female banker, and his old girl friend from thirteen years ago. I was crushed and struggling to come to grips with my new circumstances.

My husband was a handsome and well-educated man. During our earlier years of marriage, he catered to my every need, as I did his. We were inseparable until I decided to attend law school and, as I thought, find myself and find out who I really was. I had always walked in the shadow of my husband, an unidentifiable being.

I was the type of woman that a man would take home to dinner, take to special functions for representation as a nice arm-trophy piece; however, after the event was over, I would be put back on the shelf until the next time representation was required to make my husband look and feel good about his profession. During the years of marriage, it was not easy being looked upon as a timid, frail, naive, submissive, and voiceless person.

When my neighbor, Evangelist Cynthia, invited me to attend her church service, I was newly divorced and still trying to find my way as a single woman again. I had no desire to go to a church service, but my neighbor insisted that I would be blessed to hear this out-of-state preacher deliver the last night sermon of the revival. As we made our way through the church and the 3,000 other people who were attending, I ended up sitting on the second row in the middle isle of the church. I was allowed to sit there because my neighbor was the librarian of the church and an evangelist who had put much money in the building fund (she had clout).

The church was one where only the elite attended. They were condescending and didn't recognize it. Members had to conduct themselves accordingly and felt that any excitement could ruin the reputation of the church. And who would want to attend a church with all the hollering, and praising, and shouting that would deter good Christians from attending church to receive their blessings. After all, the less fortunate could attend the small store front churches down the road where they could be comfortable serving without central air conditioning or central heat.

Why am I here? I despised this type of church.

During church service, I sat very attentive as the message was being delivered. I found myself weeping and trembling almost hysterically most of the service because I suddenly began to feel lonely and alone. The message seemed to be directed at my emotional state of mind as to the loneliness I was feeling, and the emotional turmoil of being rejected as a result of the divorce and my husband walking away from the life that we had built together.

The visiting preacher, Bishop Terrence, completed his sermon and invited all who wanted prayer up to the altar. He looked behind him and beckoned the pastor of the church to bring him some anointing oil.

Immediately, when he made the altar call, his aunt, Evangelist Ann, whom I was introduced to earlier, took one of my arms and my neighbor took the other arm and led me to the altar. After looking back on the event, I was being led to slaughter like the hogs my daddy would butcher in the country.

We three, arm-in-arm, walked to the middle of the altar right in front of the pulpit. The preacher walked around the altar and stood directly in front of me. Suddenly, I felt a weakness go through my body and I began to tremble as he stared directly into my eyes. I had never felt like this before. What was this feeling? Maybe I got the Holy Ghost. I had heard of that. Bishop Terrence did not say a word for a few seconds, and then he turned away from me and walked to his left to the end of the pulpit, where he prayed, sang, and anointed with oil the individuals who requested prayer.

I stood frozen in anticipation to feel his touch on any part of my body. There was something very strange happening — I felt that if he touched me the longing, hurt, pain, fear, and lifeless feeling I had experienced in my adult life would be erased and I would be made whole again. The allure was unexplainable; the feeling that took over was more sensual than spiritual.

When he finally returned to where I was standing with the good sisters protecting me from falling, he stood for a few seconds and then passed right by me, prayed for the person standing next to me and then continued down the row to minister to the other prayer-seekers.

After he completed the altar call, with me still standing without his touch, he began to sing my favorite song. The minute I heard that song, I also heard a loud scream. The scream was coming from me, and I could not stop it from continuing to flow from my mouth.

I begin to wrestle with the women holding my arms. I broke free and ran down the aisle screaming at the top of my voice. My mind was telling me to stop, but something had a hold of me and I could not control myself.

I closed my eyes and began to cry, and ask God to save my soul. I could hear myself, but it did not sound like me. Again, I felt several hands trying to hold and control me as I wrestled to free myself. Suddenly, I felt a hand lightly touch my shoulder and heard a whisper in my ear, "God, through His Son Jesus Christ has sent me here to let you know that it is over and that you do not have to hurt anymore."

I wasn't cognizant of much after his touch, but I felt myself being dragged back to a seat with loving arms around me comforting me. I felt so tired and then drifted into a deep peaceful sleep.

When I awoke, I was sitting in the back seat of my neighbor's car, and she was driving me home. She was singing and it sounded like she was praising and thanking God for His grace and mercy in restoring my soul. I asked her how long I had been asleep. "Be quiet dear," she said; "the anointing is still upon you."

That sounded spiritual and I didn't question her.

Later, when I thought about that statement, I began to disagree with her. It was not the anointing, but it was the lust demon still upon me. Whenever I thought of that day I began to experience the same flutter in my stomach, as I would feel whenever I thought about the long and lustful nights of sex and sin.

When we arrived at my home, my neighbor helped me out of the car. She opened my door and led me to the foyer and I sat on the bench right inside the door. "I have company for dinner," she said. "If you feel better in an hour, I want you to walk down to the house and meet my company and have dinner with us. It will be an hour before I serve."

After some time, I began to compose myself and headed for my bedroom to take a shower. I had never felt so lightweight, as if I was floating on air. Then I became confused and disoriented.

After my shower, I collapsed on my bed and fell fast asleep. When I woke up it was dark outside and all the lights were off in the house. I turned on the lights and noticed that I had slept only an hour, but it seemed to have been all night.

I made my way to my closet and pulled out some jeans torn at the knees, a spaghetti strap top, a sweater, and my worn sandals.

I headed down the stairs to the kitchen to get something to eat when the doorbell rang. It was my neighbor and the visiting minister's aunt. "Are you okay?" they asked. "Yes," I said. My neighbor asked if they could come in. I led them to the kitchen and they sat while I prepared coffee. Although I did not want company because my head was hurting and I was still disoriented— I could not turn the nice church mothers away. Looking back on that evening, I should have slammed the door in their faces and said a few cuss words or better yet yelled, "Get thee away from me Satan."

Bishop Terrence's aunt began to talk about the church service, and her nephew, and how she traveled with him and some of the legal issues he was experiencing as a result of being accused by some preacher's daughter of getting her pregnant and, she was suing for child support. She wanted me to meet her nephew, the preacher, Bishop Terrence and represent him in this litigation.

I thought *this woman does not know me. Why is she telling me this man's business?* "Ms. Ann," I said, *"I cannot help you or your nephew with this issue. I do not practice family law and besides, he would have to be the one that retains me to represent him."*

"Well," she said, "I told him that you were a lawyer and he wants to meet you because there are other matters I am sure you could be of assistance to him with, because his ministry has grown so much and he needs someone that could advise him. He has been talking to other lawyers, but somehow I feel that you are the one he needs and the spirit led you to the church today."

"I do not want to sound disrespectful," I said, "but my spirit has not told me what the spirit has told you."

"Stop that blasphemy," my neighbor said. "A man of God is asking for your help and since you are going through family issues too, you should feel blessed that God has given you this opportunity to serve him. Plus, this preacher can help

"CHURCH GIRLS" the Seduction of Religion

you and bring you under his inheritance with God."

I looked at the neighbor and thought, *what is this bull crap she is giving me. I have my own inheritance with God and do not need his. Besides something is strange with this man.*

Growing up in the church in the South, I have often heard mothers of the church talking about Jezebel spirits that operated within some women, and how these women would entice men of God to perform sexual acts with them, get pregnant, and destroy the church family. I knew of at least three deacons who were relieved of their positions at the church because of outside relationships with someone other than their wives.

Before I could pour the coffee in cups and place them on the table, the aunt's cell phone rang and she got up and walked into the living room that was adjacent to the kitchen. After a brief moment, she returned and sat back down at the table. "My nephew wants to meet you tonight," she said. "He is staying at the Four Seasons and asked that we come to see him."

"I am so tired," I said, "plus I have a long day tomorrow and I just do not want to change clothes or, better yet, leave the house to meet him or anyone."

"You can go as you are and I will drive you there and bring you back," the aunt said.

Before I could think of my response, my big mouth opened and I said, "Okay, let me grab my purse."

Before we arrived at the hotel, she obviously had called

him on the telephone because he was standing outside near a rented Mercedes Benz waiting for us; dressed in jeans, tee shirt, and sneakers. When I laid eyes on him, I felt sick to my stomach.

My mind said to get out of the car and run, but my body, especially my female parts, said, "Take me to bed right now!"

He walked directly to me and put his arms around me, pulled me against him, and kissed me on the top of my head. At that point, I felt that the doors of hell had opened up and swallowed me. All of the teaching on ethics, morals, and values had disappeared. I knew I was falling into a pit of darkness. I was in lust.

I had not had a sexual encounter since my divorce, and was long overdue for passion and desperately wanted someone to show me compassion. I could feel myself sweating and about to faint from being around this man. I had not felt this way around a man in all of my life. I felt he had pulled my soul right out of my body and replaced it with a part of him. I felt all of this after experiencing his touch for the second time.

This is crazy, I thought. *How can one person have control over my emotions in less than twelve hours of my life, this has to be from God or the devil.* I wanted to believe it was God, but my upbringing in church in the South told me that I was housing that Jezebel spirit the mothers spoke about, and he was housing a lust demon that was transferred to me by his mere touch.

I believe that there are demons and I believe a touch can transfer energy that is either harmful or helpful if you possess the same or similar spirits, and that like (kindred) spirits draw each other.

I thought, if this was the Holy Ghost that I read about in the Bible, it would not make me want to dive on this man's body and make love to him right on the ground in front of all the world to see.

Obviously, I had a Jezebel spirit (a manipulating loose operating spirit) and Terrence identified me as such.

CHAPTER 5

I WAS HOOKED

"CHURCH GIRLS" the Seduction of Religion

When Bishop Terrence and I first made love, after eight months of our first meeting in front of the Four Season hotel, he had not retained me for legal representation. I received a telephone call from him to come to his hotel room to discuss the possibility of me representing him in a divorce settlement with his then wife.

When he opened the door, he was standing in a pair of jeans, no shirt and no shoes. It was late afternoon. "He leaned over and kissed me on my right cheek and the back of my neck so gently. "Do you have time to sit and wait while I finish my morning hygienic routine?" he asked. "Yes," I said.

The bishop went back into the bathroom and completed his morning task before he resurfaced again. He sat on the other side of the round table where I had sat when I first entered the room.

Not speaking or looking at me, he opened up his computer. "I want to show you something," I walked around to the side of the table where he was sitting and leaned over his shoulder. "This is the legal document I was served with last week and I just need you to review it and give me direction as to how I should handle it," he said.

"Here, sit here," he said insistently, and moved out of his seat so I could sit and read the document. All of the nervousness I was feeling when I entered the room dissipated when I sat at the computer and slowly read the document.

As I read, I took notes and found myself engulfed in the document and not aware for a few minutes of my surrounding.

When I finally looked up, he was standing by the window looking out apparently deep in thought about something. "Are you okay?" I asked. "Yes," I am just thinking, nothing in particular" he said.

I walked over to the window where he was standing and just stood there next to him. "Life is strange and has a way of failing us even when we attempt to do the right thing and make the right decisions about what direction we want our lives to go," he said. "What do you mean?" I asked. He turned to me and asked, "Are you happy with your life?" "I do not know if I could refer to my life as being a happy life but I do feel blessed," I replied.

Bishop Terrence turned and looked at me and then walked back to the table where he repositioned the computer. We talked about the legal documents for over an hour and then he asked, "Can you drop me off at the gym?" I agreed to drop him off. "Call me Terrence," he said. I looked up at him and smiled. He pulled a tee shirt from the luggage that was placed in a chair near the bed, and raised it over his head and carefully pulled it down over his body. Then, he sat on the bed and put on a pair of sneakers that was placed at the foot of the bed.

I found myself watching him and feeling panicky about being alone with him in his hotel. In an effort to control the emotional turmoil burning inside of my chest, I decided to focus my attention on the computer to take a final note before gathering my personal items to depart.

"Come here," he said. I looked up and he was standing on the other side of the table looking directly at me.

Not asking why or for what reason, I stood up and walked straight in to his arms. The trip to the gym went by the way side; we made love for many hours nonstop. I always felt that the first time was because we both needed something from each other. We both wanted to make love that day and nothing or no one would interfere with that need and want.

I felt at the time of consummating our relationship being satisfied by each other, he wanted the relationship with me to work because of my education, knowledge, and expertise in fields where it was so greatly needed for the business advancement of his ministry and not for love, marriage, and baby- in-baby carriage.

My career was moving at a fast pace when I first met him, and it was never difficult to stay focused on my work so that I could provide a decent living for myself. All of that changed after we made love for the first time that fall day in October.

There is no way to disguise my emotional state; I needed comfort and sex with only him because I trusted and cared for him. To me, having sex was my comfort and the more sex with him meant the more comfort. He needed someone to handle his legal matters and someone to have sex with him whenever he wanted.

I was like many women, whom, after a divorce or some emotional ties are broken, felt emotionally abused, stepped over, and reduced to nothing. It was easy to open up to a man who presented himself kind, showed a little compassion, and would say nice things.

It doesn't make it right... it is just a matter of fact. Unfortunately, some times the first man an abused woman encounters is a pastor who is trained to be kind, at least on the surface, because he has to be approachable in order to keep the women in his church and contributing their money.

Some female church members are taken advantage of, and the pastors should be held accountable knowing the emotional state of the parishioners. As with any other profession, preachers who willing violate the trust of the office must be liable and removed from office; the laity is a trust given by God to leaders that should be governed by a higher ethical level no matter who initiates the first move.

The church is the only institution that makes excuses by saying "well he is a man too and has needs." Notice no other institution takes this stance. Even if the male is exonerated, the institution in spirit doesn't lower its ethics by verbalizing we'll make an exception.

Terrence spellbound me, that at the beginning of the relationship I would have jumped off a building for him because of my deep and never ending love for him. He was my life, my god, my heart, and the breath that I breathed. I loved him more than life itself.

The sexual encounters continued as a ritual between us: We both would leave church, go to dinner, take long baths together, foreplay, and engaged in hot sex all night. Then, morning into the afternoon, take a nap, cuddle up like two lovers, and at 4 p.m. I would leave the room so he could study for the night's sermon. At this point in the relationship, I might expect a telephone call at 2 a.m. demanding that I "bring my body to him" for a quickie before he fell asleep. He claimed that the sex would help him relax so he could sleep a few hours before boarding the plane to travel to his next destination. I was always happy to accommodate his wishes.

My obsession and lust for Terrence altered my personality and adversely affected my relationship with family and friends, and jeopardized my professional life. I was madly drowning in lust.

On any given day, I would travel by car for a maximum of five hours to attend the end of church service, have sex, get back in the car, and drive home and then have just enough time to shower, change clothes, and go to court.

If Terrence was attending church in any state within the five hours radius regardless of the number of days he would be ministering in that state, I would make sure that I was there just to be near him even if we did not have sex. It was enough to look at him and inhale the same air as he did.

I thought that I was giving Terrence support by being there for him whenever he ministered as a guest preacher; after all, his church members could not attend service each time he ministered outside of his church state being that the church was in another time zone.

I would sit in church and observe his every move. The movement of his body, especially his hands, and the many eye-to-eye contacts we exchanged while he was in the pulpit would make me twist in my seat. I felt like I would have an orgasm right inside of the church.

I discovered that if Terrence and I made love after he delivered his sermon, the sex would be something to die for. I felt that way at the beginning of the relationship with the bishop, and I am still not completely sure but believe it to be true.

I lusted for Terrence, a lot; I had fallen deeply in love and lust with this man but he did not love me back.

As time went on, my life was conflicted and intertwined to his. Sometimes I second guessed the involvement with him and wondered what I had gotten myself involved with. Was I possessed by a lust demon or was I just a "booty call" for him whenever he came into the state or whenever he decided he wanted to experience sex with me?

On many occasions, Terrence would fly me to the city or state where he was appearing and we would have a night of passion. Afterwards, both of us would board separate airplanes and head our detached ways. He said that was a way of keeping us both out of trouble.

I really loved this man and I would have spent my life with him, needing and wanting no one or nothing else. However, I knew God was not going to give him to me or me to him and was not going to bless our union in anyway because both he and I knew better; the relationship had started out wrong and for the wrong reasons. He needed a lawyer, I needed sex, and that induced a false sense of believing that I could love and be loved again without any strings attached. I knew that God was not pleased, and we both would suffer as a result of the disobedience, but our flesh would not let us stop.

Terrence was aware of my needs, desires, and how his touch and stares affected me mentally and physically whenever he was near me. At first, he was financially supportive and provided me with any finances that he thought that I needed or wanted, and for whatever reason, including paying his legal fees. Later, about a year into the relationship, he began to pull back on his finances because he thought my workload was too heavy, and there was no time to accommodate his many legal needs, attend church outside of the state, and manage other clients. He wanted me to close up my office and travel with him, taking care of all of his legal issues and those of his colleagues (preachers).

When I refused to agree to be submissive, he became angry and disappointed with my legal services, and therefore refused to pay legal fees or provide any financial support to a life in which he made me accustomed, he thought. He began to want legal services free of charge for him and his colleagues, as if I owed him something or his control over me was so great that I would do anything for him or his preacher friends just because he demanded it.

Terrence often stated that we were both alike when it came to making money. Once, following a meeting with Terrence and several of his colleagues who had plans of opening a radio station, he wanted to meet with me afterwards to recap on the final financial details. "We are so much alike," he said. "How so?" I asked. "Money is the primary drive in both of our lives, followed by sex and a healthy relation," he said.

This statement was not true as to how I felt about Terrence. However, I could not reveal to him that I would give up my life just to be with him twenty-four hours every day if he could only assure me that the relationship would work. And that I would not be giving up a life that I had built for myself just so that he could progress and then drop me off at the nearest trash dump. After several years of being emotionally involved, he had the audacity to tell me that the major connection between us was based mostly on money and sex. This statement really hurt deeply.

During many of our pillow talks when I happened to stay over in his room following our love making sessions, which were quite often in the beginning of our relationship. I believe that Terrence wanted to reveal his weakness for women to me. And the pillow talk was his way of slowly opening up and carefully monitoring my response to seek my reactions.

He would casually discuss his relationships with other women; however, it was always odd to me that he would risk his ministry to have a relationship with married women. It was also odd how he would discuss those relationships with me as if it was normal, and how he would identify these women, with most of them being wives of preachers, daughters, sisters, or aunts of preachers whose churches he would minister at on a frequent basis. He exhibited no respect for another man's house.

He knew that I was an independent woman in the business world; however, spiritually I was dependent on him to counsel me about my soul salvation, and I could not understand why he felt comfortable discussing other women with me if it did not have any personal or legal relevance. He knew I would never leave him as long as he was taking care of my spiritual and sexual needs. He was worse than any drug; he was an addiction to me and I needed treatment. Only God through His Son Jesus Christ could provide that treatment—if only I could let him go.

Following the talks at night with Terrence, I felt dirty, sinful and spiritually void, which often gave me the thoughts of perhaps revisiting the baptism pond where I was first baptized at the age of twelve. To ask God to take away all of the filth that I felt and renew me, wash me clean, take away all of my sins with this man and allow my redemption.

I was never a "hypocrite"; either I would love him, cherish him, make love to him, or just leave him and never look back. My motto has always been never to go backward in anything that I do or experience in life. The conundrum was could I do it with this man—he was definitely my ruler, and I his servant.

He was an enigma; in many ways, he was a good and compassionate man when I met him and up to the last day that I spoke to him, I believed that I would never look back. However, I realized early in the relationship that he exhibited such a disrespect for women, (even though he was born into a family of preachers and evangelists), whether single or married, which always confused me.

After a few years into the relationship with Terrence, his ministry and assets began to grow. I was very happy about the growth of his ministry because he was a very anointed and powerful preacher and teacher.

To avoid any gossip or harmful repercussions for him in the church world because of our relationship, even though we thought we were being secretive and careful, I felt it was inappropriate to sleep all night in his arms. In addition to sleep in the same hotel or hotel room when I visited him outside of the state of Pennsylvania or when he came to Pennsylvania to minister.

I realize that seemed strange, since I had already sinned by having sex with him; however, I was still able to believe that I had some sense of respect for myself and for his ministry. In addition, I could never face myself in the mirror after having made love to him during the entire time of our relationship. It seems that mentally, the scripture of *"Touch not my anointed"* would rivet in my spirit every time we made love, and God had warned me many times that He would intervene if I continued to be disobedient.

Not once during our relationship have I ever doubted that Terrence was one of God's chosen people. I, on the other hand, forgot that I too, was one of God's chosen and allowed myself to drown in carnality. Like so many women who give up their spiritual identity because of sin but men will never walk away from who they are in God. I was foolish.

"Why could I not stop sinning with one of God's chosen people?"

From the date of becoming personally and professionally involved with Terrence, he was in a divorce battle and fighting issues of alimony and child support.

CHAPTER 6

FROM SINNER TO SINFUL

The weather was just turning warm. I sat at my desk wondering if I could ever tell this man of God that he was out of my spirit for good. In my moments of regret, I knew the relationship was wrong; but for the most part, I remained under his spell. Lost in thought and daydreaming of Terrence, I let my mind and body float into the memories of the many nights of passion, but avoided thinking about the nights I wanted to flee from his room after making love to him because of the shame I experienced. Anytime or at any place, no matter when and where I thought of Terrence, I began to feel a pulsation in my stomach that radiated to the most sensitive female part of my body. It was as if I was experiencing an orgasm with actual physical contact.

Tonight Terrence was the guest speaker and headliner for the summer revival at a very prominent church in Philadelphia that seated over 2,500 people. He did not accept the invitation every year but when he did, I made all efforts, within my control, to clear my calendar so that he could get all of my undivided attention while he was in the city.

Terrence had not notified me as to the time he would be flying into the city for tonight's service. This was not out of the ordinary because the sponsoring church always assigned a designated driver to transport him to his hotel, and assured the accommodations were perfect.

"Ms. Davis, Ms. Davis, are you okay?" My secretary interrupted my uncomfortable memories. She was standing in front of my desk with a legal folder that was prepared for a deposition in one hour. "I have all of your requested documents in separate folders and tagged for quick reference," she said.

"CHURCH GIRLS" the Seduction of Religion

"Thanks Tonya, you are the best, and by the way, how long were you standing in front of my desk?"

"Long enough for me to guess that your soul is not at ease with whatever you are thinking."

Tonya was a sixty-five-year-old church mother that I hired when I arrived in Pennsylvania. She was very responsible and loyal to me and helped me to find my way around, and to locate my suburban home outside of Philadelphia.

Tonya was from the South and we had grown up with similar religious backgrounds; we were taught to attend church on Sunday, go to Bible study on Wednesday, choir rehearsal on Tuesday night, and visit the sick on Saturday.

Tonya was my conscience during times that I did not realize I did not have a conscience or exhibited moral values and ethics when it came to this "great man of God."

I suspected that Tonya had once been involved in a situation similar to mine, because I would observe her on many occasions while I was on the phone talking to him, watching me with a very distant and sad look on her face.

I have always known that my involvement with this bishop was a mistake. I also knew that the only way to get out of this relationship was to pray that God would remove him from my spirit. I began to believe in order for this to occur I must sever all contact with Terrence, put distance between us, and refuse to communicate with him in any form. Easier said than done.

I finally pulled myself out of my chair and pushed it back so that I could stand and gathered my thoughts, before I committed a negligent act of representing a client who had just lost her mother as a result of hospital negligence. I understood the importance of representing my clients and affording them the best representation that one could give, even though very few of the clients could afford to pay legal fees.

Most of my days were committed to working with nonpaying clients and the weekends were dedicated to feeding the homeless and, assisting veterans and their families with locating housing. The weekends were the only times in my life that gave me great pleasure and helped me falsely to believe that I was not such a sinner in the eyes of God.

I walked out of my office, and headed for the front entrance of the office building. I was already late and I knew that my client was getting panicky because she had telephoned the office and inquired into my expected time of arrival.

I began to feel a strong flutter in my stomach, and then my cell phone started to ring.

I looked at the phone before I answered and realized that it was Terrence. There was a strange and very unusual connection between us.

"Hello," I said.
"Where are you?" he responded." This was his routine question.
"I am on my way to a deposition and I am running very late, can I call you back?"

"My flight will be in at 4 p.m. and I need to discuss the New Jersey property matter with you before I leave for church," he said.

I knew there was no property matter needing to be discussed prior to church service tonight, and I was aware that this was a call for a quick, last-minute sexual encounter with his *lawyer* and *concubine so he could relax and prepare for service.* He knew that the only thing he needed to do was to call me and I would freely give him the sex. I deceived myself into adhering to his demands (I convinced myself that I was important to him). He perceived asking for sex as a right, and it was the woman's duty to perform.

When I heard his smooth enticing (many called it anointed) baritone voice over the phone beckoning me to come forward and do my duties as a dedicated sister of the church, ready and willing to be of service to such a great man of God as he, I automatically replied, "I will be there hopefully by 5 p.m."

Before I entered my vehicle I stood on the sidewalk and looked around, deep in thought about him and my life, I thought to myself, "I am in love with a man of the cloth and unconditionally loving him regardless of what I know about his sexual addiction and his women, me being one of them. How could I think of leaving him because he saved me that day, many years ago, from my pitiful self?"

My life was in such shambles when Terrence and I became intimate; he was kind, and encouraged me to move forward even though the level of our involvement was a conflict of interest.

I would resolve to end the relationship and then he would call and my "resolve" melted.

CHAPTER 7

THE SPIRIT OF JEZEBEL

I had learned a lot about unholy relationships between pastors and parishioners during the nine years of my affair with Bishop Terrence.

One thing that rather amused me about the church is the fact that the church world labeled, and acknowledged the description of women connected to the preacher in an intimate sense of the word as "worthless." Church members know the wife of a preacher as the first lady, and no one really discuss the facts and reality of a "second lady" lurking in the background, nor the "*Madam*" in third place when it comes to the pastor's unholy relationships.

The first lady of the pastor, which is usually the wife who pledged her vows to the preacher in a holy setting, is obedient, submissive, and comfortable in her position with the preacher as her husband. She is often blind to his unfaithfulness and hides her pain for the sake of remaining in that position and enjoying all of the amenities of being the wife, including bearing his name, using the credit cards for her shopping sprees and standing beside him on the pulpit for all the world to know that he chose her.

The second lady knows her place; she knows when to attend certain church services, when to volunteer to serve the preacher at conventions and anniversary dinners. When the time is right to accept the position of choir director as an appointed position per the preacher's instruction, or when to relieve the secretary of her position so that she can manage the church office and the preacher's schedule. She is the one all church members usually gossip about.

The Madam is the lady of the night, the escort after the church convention nightly services ends. She stays out of sight during the daily holy activities, conferences, and workshops unless she holds the position of second lady. The Madam is the one that has to endure the small talk between the preacher and his first lady, while she is intimately stroking the preacher during his attempt to have phone sex with his first lady. Who is dying to have an orgasm because she knows he is going to give someone an orgasm while he is at the convention, so why should she not get hers too.

The Madam lies there as the preacher pledges his undying love to his first lady and has to endure the chatter between the preacher and the first lady. It begins with the preacher saying, "What will I do without you these next five days," and the old "goodnight baby I miss you and wish you were here." The Madam is the lucky and rewarded one of them all at the church conventions, because she is highly compensated financially for a few minutes of nightly service to the preacher. The Madam of the evening gets to shop every day, sleep during church service, dress up at night, and perform the "quickie sex acts" before the preacher returns to the room to lie with the second lady.

Another less flattering term, especially as the sex world refers to it as "the bottom whore." This is one who happens to be the preacher's center of attention for a specific purpose, day and time in the life and growth of his ministry — one who has told her friends of her undying love and loyalty to him and her total purpose in life is that of serving him, following him, and coming at his beckoning call.

She is the one that prays every day that God will prick his heart, show him of her undying love, and choose her so that she would one day become his 1st lady for the entire world to see.

I know the script very well because not only had I been the "second lady" to Terrence without the duties of being the descriptive second lady of the church, I was also a "bottom whore" and his "Madam."

Terrence was a man that demanded perfection out of his women. He referred to perfection as that of being submissive and catering to the need of the man. For nine years of our relationship, I endeavored to be the perfect woman in his life. I put all of my needs aside so that I could assure his happiness, wealth and advancement in the corporate world.

Towards the end of our relationship, Terrence became very distant with me. He found excuses as to why we could not see each other during birthdays or holidays. He found excuses as to why he did not want me to travel anymore to meet him in certain cities.

The trips to Philadelphia and surrounding areas became less frequent within the final years of our relationship. Not only were the trips less frequent, the visits to my bed after the nightly services were beginning to decrease.

When questioned about the drastic changes in the Philadelphia visits, more specifically, our personal relations, he summarized the changes as being a result of the high demands on his schedule from ministers throughout the country and overseas, the growth of his ministry, and a vow that he had made to God. He had vowed to God that he would not continue to fornicate with me or anyone else.

Terrence's distant behavior to me became challenging. I began to withdraw myself from him and began to refuse his telephone calls. The phone calls and the visits slowly decreased from one month to three months and then six months before we visited each other. I began to turn my focus back on my life before Terrence and was pleased with my daily progress. "He has found another female project," I thought and that makes me feel comforted to know that I got some help from someone, anyone as far as it concerned his personal problems, even though I missed him terribly.

On his next visit to Philadelphia, he was invited to minister at a summer revival in Philadelphia and a convention in New Jersey during the same week. He said that he agreed to the invitations so that he could spend some time with me and that he was tired of me whining about needing him. "Right," the new female project must have dumped him," I thought.

Terrence was only supposed to minister for one day at the revival in Philadelphia and one day at the convention in New Jersey, but it ended up that he was asked to minister in Philadelphia a second night after he ministered in New Jersey.

Terrence sent an email to me the day before his arrival in Philadelphia and informed me that he would be ministering in Philadelphia the first night, and wanted to know if I was going to attend. He also inquired about my attendance in New Jersey. I found this strange that he would question my attendance; after all, I was his number one follower. It was not until the second night when he ministered in New Jersey that I understood why he asked if I was going to attend church.

I was not emotionally equipped for the days to follow the revival in New Jersey – it was the end of the week when

Terrence would minister. This had not been a good time for me because I had been in meetings all week addressing problems and more problems. I had listened to clients discuss how financially insolvent they were but still wanted my services, responded to messages from disgruntled employees, and tried to comfort clients who had little chance of winning their cases. Some wanted me to say a prayer before we met — asking God to lead and guide my footsteps, while others wanted my destruction.

To top all of the stress, I had to see Terrence that night, attend church, and after service pretend, I was happy to see him because I needed him in my life more than he could ever imagine. This would be very difficult for me because I could not conceal my feelings about the rumors that have been floating around about his indiscretions with married women.

I rushed home, which was over twenty miles from the city. After traveling and battling traffic, I just wanted to sink down on the floor and go to sleep. I was in a carpool so the twenty-five miles seemed like two hundred miles in traffic.

After what seemed like an eternity, I finally entered my home and made a conscious effort to convince myself to shower, put on my church attire, and feed my puppy, who surely felt unloved and forgotten by me. I did not have much time to catch up on any of my work or to attend to my house or my animal the way a normal person should do.

During the entire ride home, I had mixed emotions about seeing Terrence. It had been my day to drive for the carpool, which took an extra 25 minutes to arrive home. I really struggled with the idea of attending church and had every intention to do so, but I was just too tired to pull myself together and put on church attire.

I think all of the procrastination was a result of not wanting to be bothered with his lies and deception. I knew he would be in the city for three nights; if I missed this one night, he should understand, because he is the main reason I am mentally drained, deranged, and behind in all of my work. I decided to go to bed.

A woman sometimes makes a common mistake by giving a man precedence when he should be second; a man seldom will ever sacrifice his career for a woman.

At 12 midnight, the phone next to my bed rang, awakening me out of a deep sleep. He was on the other end of the line yelling and screaming.

"I know you are in the house and I know you have someone else in there with you," he yelled. "If you do not open this door, I will burn down this house with you and the person in it."

"Where are you?" I asked.

"I am outside of your door and you better open this door," he said. Anxious and nervous, I tried to get out of the bed and fell flat on the floor. This man was outside my house yelling on the phone and all of the Holy Ghost filled neighbors had heard him preach, and I was sure that they had heard rumors of the preacher's relationship with me.

While peeling myself off the floor and preparing for the confrontation with Terrence, I thought, "He must be spying on me." He knows that I am in a carpool and I do interact with men other than him but not sexually. I had introduced him to the men in the carpool, and he knew that I worked at home sometimes and there were men that I worked with. I made my way down the stairs and opened the front door. He was standing there, still dressed in the clothes he had worn to church. Evidently, he had not gone back to his hotel room to changed clothes, but had come straight to my house.

As I was walking down the stairs, I said to myself again, "Has this man been spying on me." I do carpool some days and why would he automatically assume another man was in my bed.

I stood in the doorway and said, "What is wrong with you; have you lost your mind?"

"If you have someone in this house, there won't be you or a house to talk about," he said, and pushed his way into the room. "Sit down," he said, "I mean sit down."
"Terrence there is no one in this house but me and the puppy," I said.

I sat on the sofa and was afraid to move because he was standing over me like an angry animal that had rabies or some other form of mad animal disease.

He headed upstairs to my bedroom to look around; I started to follow him but he placed his hand on the rail to prevent me from coming behind him. As he was walking up the stairs, he said, "I cannot trust you and I know that you are a liar and will cheat on me at the drop of a hat."

I thought to myself, *How he could have delivered a sermon that night, laid hands on people, and spoke under the anointing, and then come over here acting like the devil that just descended from hell.*

I went to the kitchen and made some coffee (this gave me a moment to strategize in case he got crazier). First, I thought about getting out of the house before he could try to kill me. I was afraid that there would be no way to calm him down, and I would need a route of escape. I thought maybe I could open the balcony door, jump off, and try not to break my neck, sneak through the garage and ram the garage door with the car because he would probably grab me before I got the garage door open with the electrical door opener.

Then I thought, "Maybe it would be better to remove all of my clothes and entice him into having sex with me to calm him down. After all, it had worked in the past when he became angry and upset with me.

Terrence came down the stairs as I was taking the final piece of cotton pajama bottoms off. I could not face him because I did not want him to see the fear in my face.

"Baby, what is wrong?" I asked, standing there just as naked as the day I was born. "Okay, examine me for signs of another man, I said. This is good for this relationship. Perhaps we both should exam each other," I said.

As I turned to face him, his eyes were scanning my body.

He opened his arms and I walked into them. Terrence undressed and we found ourselves on the floor lost in lust and sin. His lovemaking was violent that night as he pressed me into the hard wood floor with such force; pounding my naked body until we both were drenched in sweat. I wanted to scream because of all the pain that I was feeling both mental and physical, but I refused to give him the satisfaction.

That night as we lie in bed holding each other, he made a feeble attempt to dedicate his love and devotion to me and promised never to leave me again. "I am sorry for leaving you so long and for so many other things that I have done to mess up this relationship," he said. "Bernadette, I have really caused a lot of problems in my ministry and my personal life. I know you have heard rumors about me and my relationship with Reverend Tony's wife," he said. I turned my back to him and pushed my body into his. I laid beside him and listened for over an hour as he poured out his heart to me, revealing his relationships with married women, more specifically the wife of one of his friends. I really began to feel sorry for him and thought of ways for him to get some help.

"Are you really that crazy?" I asked. What! He said. "Crazy, a nut, a fruit cake like in needing medication." I raised up from the bed and turned to face him so I could look directly into his eyes. "Terrence, what were you thinking when you slept with this man's wife. To top it off, why did you sleep with her in the same city?" I said. "Terrence, you slept with a woman in the city in which she lives and in the hotel the church paid for," I said.

"I am disgusted with you all the time screwing up and then running back to me to clean up all your mess. Damn, I cannot believe you did that, but then again I can because you definitely are a whoremonger," I said, and turned my back to him in an attempt to get some sleep. "So this is why you made this outrageous scene tonight because you really are the guilty

"CHURCH GIRLS" the Seduction of Religion

party," I thought. Before I drifted off to sleep, I heard him say, "I am here aren't I." He knew my fear of being alone and he knew how to and when to say the words that would secure me from that thought.

The next morning I left him at the house and went to the office. Later that day he called and said that there was a change of locations for tonight's service. The New Jersey convention had moved the location from the hotel to the church for the last night of the convention.

I promised him that I would definitely come to service and would be there to support him. At 6pm, when I again glanced at the clock on my desk, it was obvious that time had slipped away from me. It had taken me longer to prepare for my next day appointments, and I knew that church service was scheduled for 7:00pm and he would be entering onto the pulpit at 8:00pm following praise and worship.

I knew that I would be facing an outrage if I did not make it to service tonight and this time, he just might follow through on last night's threats.

My home was too far away to travel to change clothes for church so I had to ascertain as to whether I would go home, and take my chances and show up around 10:00pm for church. Alternatively, I could wear the same clothes that I had been in all day, or change into a pair of dress shorts and a blazer that I kept at the office. I opted to change into the shorts and blazer and then rushed out of the office building and headed for the church.

When I finally arrived at the church, I could not find a

parking space because it was so crowded. I drove around looking for over ten minutes in an attempt to locate a space as close to the church as possible. I was not familiar with this part of New Jersey and had never visited this church before so I was driving around blindly.

Before I could find a parking space and park the Mercedes Benz, he had purchased for my birthday the previous year, my phone beeped around 7:55pm. Terrence had sent me a text message "You are nothing but a deceitful liar, and I just don't want to deal with you anymore. If you are not here by 8:30pm just forget about coming. Where are you?"

Terrence seemed to be stressed about something and I did not know why. I could not understand why it was so important to be in church tonight; I began to get a suspicious feeling about the text message and about the motive behind the message. It appeared to me that he is timing my arrival for a reason only he knows, or pretending to care, I thought.

His words ignited anger and fear simultaneously as I reflected on his actions the previous evening and I sent back a message: "F......YOU TOO! And I hope God kills your sinful ass while you are up there preaching and laying hands on people. You're less than a man, asshole."

I did not hear back from him again, and finally after driving around another five minutes I was able to locate a parking spot. I entered the church lobby shaken and angry at the verbal abuse. He was getting good at the abuse and it appears I have been his target for the last three months. I walked up to the door of the church and entered the lobby. I made my way to the restroom to freshen up before I went into the sanctuary. I stood outside the entrance of the sanctuary for a few minutes in hopes that I could compose myself long enough to find a seat in the back of the church, to hide from his stares. No such luck.

When I entered the sanctuary, he had not yet entered the pulpit. The back seats of the sanctuary were occupied — so the efficient and dedicated ushers seated me in one of the five empty seats on the front row, right in front of the pulpit next to several unfamiliar faces. "This is got to be a joke," I thought. As I sat down, I began to look around to see if there were any familiar faces because I definitely needed to see someone that I knew.

I spotted several evangelists and other females that I had seen in some of the other church services throughout the area. None of these women had ever missed Terrence's services and I wondered. Before I could comfortably adjust my body in my seat, I felt someone seated directly behind me touch me on the shoulder. As I slightly turned, I recognized that the person touching me was 1st lady Cecil, the wife of one of the preachers sitting on the pulpit. "Why she isn't sitting on the front row is a mystery. "I knew you would be here because the only time I see you in church is when Bishop Terrence comes to visit this area," she said. Little did she know that I just saw her husband a few days ago in my office crying about how unhappy he is with her old butt. She needs to attend to her own affairs and stop worrying about my soul, I thought.

I touched the woman's hand gently and turned my attention to getting comfortable for the sermon. As an instant reflex, I crossed my legs and laid my purse next to my left ankle. By this time, Terrence had entered the pulpit and was being introduced. Not aware of my attire and its tendency to move as my body moved, the short set, which reached below my knees, had suddenly risen to my thighs and I was showing more skin than I should have been showing in a church setting.

Realizing what was happening, I began to uncross my legs, and in the act of doing so, I suddenly felt Terrence staring at me. I was too nervous to look up at him just standing a few feet away, but I could feel him staring. I forced myself to look up at the pulpit and noticed that Terrence was in fact, without doubt in my mind, staring directly at me along with several other ministers on the pulpit, all of whom I knew personally. Appearing to be in shock or angry, Terrence paused for a brief moment and then proceeded. "Where was I? Oh, I think I was about to read the scripture," he said.

Fool, I thought, *everyone is looking at you looking at me. That is where you are.*

Terrence truly appeared confused and it seemed like he stood there for an eternity trying to compose himself. After a few seconds, he collected himself and then looked right into my eyes before addressing the congregation and pulpit guests. "Before I proceed and get to the text, I need to do something I have never done before," he said. Terrence left the pulpit, and all of the pulpit guest preachers followed him. The entire pulpit had disappeared and did not return for five minutes while the entire congregation was sitting wondering what was going on. The choir thought it fitting to sing a praise and worship song, with the help of the congregation, to break the silence.

First lady Cecil attempted once again to make small talk with me but I pretended I was reading scriptures from the small bible that I kept in my purse. After a few seconds of trying to get my attention she settled herself back in her seat and began to gossip. I am sure the gossip was about me.

After five minutes, Terrence returned to the pulpit followed by the guest preachers. "The Holy Spirit told me to anoint the entire pulpit and then instruct all of the pulpit ministers to walk out among the congregation and touch and anoint each and everyone who attended church service tonight," he said. I did not question his act or doubt that the Holy Spirit had instructed him.

I had invited staff members from the office to attend service that night. However, some of the women in the office had already decided to attend the convention in New Jersey after attending the previous service in Philadelphia, and decided to carpool. They were all very excited about having hands laid on them and I was excited for them. All of the staff in the office knew that Terrence was my client, and I am sure some of them suspected he was more than a client, since whenever he came to the office, the door would be locked with a *DO NOT DISTURB* sign on the door.

I sat in my seat for a few minutes and observed Terrence laying hands on preachers in the pulpit before I stood up and left the church sanctuary. I knew he would think I intentionally wore this outfit and deliberately made this attempt to distract him. He later confirmed that he thought my actions were calculative and as a solution to the distraction, he decided to anoint the church rather than come down from the pulpit and cast the demons out of me.

As I walked out of the sanctuary into the church lobby

I thought, "how could I stoop so low as to allow myself to come into the house of God and act as if I was Satan's child, and how could I allow this man to dictate my acts and actions and disrespect God like this." I kept telling myself it was not intentional. He is a man of God ministering and giving hope to the hopeless and I, a sinner, am swearing and cursing him before he enters the pulpit to minister to the people who are here in church to hear "thus saith the Lord." I had finally sealed my fate with God, I thought.

If I thought that the scene inside the church was the grand finale I was deeply mistaken.

Deep in thought, I decided to leave the church before I lost all dignity and respect for myself. As I passed through the lobby of the church, I had to walk by all of the memorabilia tables that were displayed throughout the lobby area. At the end of the display row, when I thought that I had escaped everyone with whom I was acquainted, I had the pleasure of passing by the table guarded by sisters Edith and Roberta. I turned my head away from them pretending to read some of the flyers that were taped to the walls surrounding the display areas at the front entrance of the lobby.

My intent was to hurry pass them and ignore their presence. Before I got to the exit of the lobby, I felt someone grabbing my right hand. "Oh, hello Ms. Davis," Sister Roberta said. "How are you ladies tonight?" I said with a loving and kind smile. "Have you heard the news that Deacon Snitzer announced from the pulpit tonight?"

I stopped abruptly and said, "What news?"

"About Bishop Terrence and Sister Josalin, his fiancé,' Sister

"CHURCH GIRLS" the Seduction of Religion

Roberta said. "You should see her ring."

Stunned, I said, "No! This is the first I've heard."

"Well," Sister Edith said, "*We just figured you would know.*" She paused and gave me a knowing smile, "*Since you and Bishop Terrence are so close and all…I mean, you do take care of all his legal affairs…*" Barely able to speak, I asked, "*So who is the lucky girl again?*"

"She's bishop's Gluten's daughter from the church across town."

My knees were so weak I thought I might fold up on the floor. I finally managed to say, "*Well, I hope they will be very happy. Now excuse me ladies, I have some urgent business,*" I said, and made my exit through the lobby door.

I had known for years that there had been quite a few other women in his life, which was the main cause of the distance between us, and the strain on what appeared to be a relationship between a man and a woman. Throughout the years, I had endured his possessive and childish behavior whenever he came to the city to minister. I was neither the first nor the only. But I had always felt our relationship was somehow special because I was his "confidante."

I was all too aware of how easily women were drawn to him, and how he did not discourage them. I felt that if he could convince me, an educated and successful businesswoman to become his mistress and then concubine after his divorce, then no other female would stand a chance against the education, knowledge, and the anointing of this man. He would dupe them too.

I thought about the female wearing his ring. I was familiar with her father's ministry and knew she lived in New Jersey with her parents. I also knew that she had only a high school education, worked part-time in a fast food restaurant, and a beauty parlor part-time on the weekend. She was thirty-five years old. Good pick of the litter, I thought, the daughter of a bishop, and what better way to expedite your fame and fortune in the church world other than that of holy matrimony with the daughter of a renowned bishop from New Jersey.

At least Terrence is not prejudice when it comes to the type of woman he chooses to get involved with. All women are fair game to him if he sees a benefit in it for him. "A single woman? I wonder what other qualifications were criteria for this one was beside the daughter of a preacher." I said aloud.

What a Joke!

As I was walking to my car, I began to have flashbacks of the conversations during the many nights of pillow talks with Terrence. All of his casually mentioning the number of proposals he had received from certain ministers regarding the marriage into their family, and the amenities that he would receive as a result of the marriage were obviously true. Although the conversations seemed to be in passing, I began to look back at the seriousness of the conversations and got sick to my stomach. What a Night!

Even though, at that moment, I didn't think I would ever again want anything to do with him, I was still humiliated and heartbroken.

When I got in my car and headed towards the turnpike, I realized how tired I was from activities of the day and the mental stress of coming to church this late at night. Tired, hurt and frustrated, I thought it best that I locate a hotel and check in for the night.

Before going to the hotel I stopped by the nearest convenient store and picked up a few personal items so that I could soak my tired body and get some rest. I was so exhausted I fell last asleep a soon as I got out of the shower and found my way to the bed.

I had slept only a few hours before I heard the telephone ring. Terrence was on the other end of the telephone asking me why I didn't pick up the telephone when he called me earlier. "Are you asleep?" he inquired. "Yes I was asleep and I intend to go back to sleep as soon as you hang up this telephone," I replied. "Did you make it home?" he asked. "No I decided to stay at a hotel instead because I am just too tired to drive all the way home and then back into the city by the time I have to see the first appointment, which is early," I said.

We talked for a few minutes before he asked what hotel I was staying in. "I want to apologize for what happened tonight and the text message that I sent. I thought you were ignoring me and disrespecting me," he said. "Terrence, I have had a long day and I am tired of playing games, you need to grow up," I said. "Listen Bernadette, I needed you to speak with a couple of ministers tonight about the project in New Jersey; I had made a promise to them that you would be at church and afterwards we could meet with them to go over a few issues with the project before closing on the deal," he said.

"Terrence, I am tired of you volunteering my services to your fellow whoremongers and, I am tired of dealing with your Whorers and your lying behind self," I said. "Why are you bothering me this early in the morning anyways; where's gutter whore girlfriend—she didn't feel like servicing you tonight? Seeing him pretend I was the only woman in his life filled me with utter disgust…he is such a darn hypocrite.

"Oh! I forgot, she had to go home with daddy and mama because she is too pure do things like that," I said.

He wanted nothing to do with my conversation about his other woman and glossed over every word I said.

"Bernadette, what is the address? You either give it to me or I will make tomorrow a very difficult and embarrassing day for you," he said. "Let's just have breakfast and talk about this; please give me the address," he pleaded.

Eventually I gave him the name and address of the hotel, and in 30 minutes, he was knocking on the door. Even though I had been devastated hearing about his fiancé, I chose to believe that there was some sort of misunderstanding. I was in denial and in a weakened state. I wished to GOD I had the strength to walk away from him, but where would I go? Looking back, I understand there was an open door that I was too afraid to go through for fear of being alone, so I settled for being blinded by my needs.

This would have been a good night for phone sex instead of wrestling with the awkwardness of looking in his face as his lies slithered off his tongue, I thought.

I lie in bed until I heard him knock on the door. I had not brought any pajamas with me because I had no intent of staying in a hotel when I left the office, so I had to sleep without any clothes on. I located a towel, wrapped it around me, and went to the door to let him in. He walked inside of the room and I walked into his arms. We never made it to breakfast.

Terrence was not the only sick one in this relationship; I was equally imbalanced and decided to quit lying to myself. Although I avoided addressing this for a very long time, but there was no escaping the inevitable… I knew I had to look at the woman in the mirror with all of her scars and broken dreams… the woman who desperately wanted to be loved and accepted.

This scenario had become a routine for me and I could not control myself. I had told myself earlier that I was stopping at the hotel because I was tired when the primary reason for being in New Jersey was in hopes that he would contact me, and invite himself over to make love to me.

I had become delusional in believing that I was somehow special to him and he truly had the capability to love me. I wanted to believe that I had not been placed aside in his life— nor replaced by others who could propel him further in his ministry more than I could.

CHAPTER 8

THE BEGINNING OF
THE END

"CHURCH GIRLS" the Seduction of Religion

I have always wondered why the 1st lady of the church turns her head to the indiscretions of her husband, and accepts all of the emotional abuse openly displayed by him with other women, especially women in the congregation. She has to have knowledge of the indiscretions and realize that church members discuss the minister's indiscretions and wonder why she does not take a stand on the issue. The 1st lady also has to understand that she is accountable to the church members, especially the women. Turning the other cheek while her husband is committing sexual acts with women in the congregation is not a sign of being accountable. She has to ask herself, which is more important, the title or bringing awareness to the sexual abuse of the women in the congregation and a solution to stopping this abuse.

From the date of becoming personally and professionally involve with Bishop Terrence, he was still married and fighting issues of alimony and child support in court. The gossip club in church has the job of putting out rumors on ministers. On the subject of the church rumors (which I later realized were true), Terrence's portfolio was centered on the marriage irreconcilable differences between him and his then wife.

Terrence's problems stemmed from his fathering two children out of wedlock while he was married. Both baby mama's were daughters of preachers.

Terrence and I had many discussions on this particular topic of child support, and each time he never followed through on any of the advice that he was given, which resulted in the judge raising the child support payments above what the average father would have to pay. I think that is why he always invited me to church conventions after we met. He knew how hard the legal system is on father's who do not pay child support.

I was caught up in the middle of his legal issues with his women and that made me nervous when it came to petitions for nonpayment of child support. I wanted to believe him when he said that he had always and timely tendered all child and alimony support as ordered by the court; however, with him it was hard to believe anything he said.

Terrence was not alone when it came to a preacher fathering children out of wedlock (it's a growing club), he just happened to get caught and exposed sooner than some of the other preachers in his circle. My guess is that the other preachers, at least the majority of them fathered children with women in their congregation and were sworn to secrecy.

Talking to Terrence after a heated night of uninhibited sex has always brought out the truth in him. He has always seemed to be quite the chatterbox when he tasted and feasted on my body as a dessert item, which was every time we made love. He definitely was never limited to what new sex positions he taught me each time we made love or inhibited about what he did to my body to make me happy that made me experience orgasm after orgasm. I knew I was not the first female to enjoy this pleasure, even though I wanted desperately to believe it.

The conflict I have always had as to my place in Terrence's life is that I never knew where I fit into his life.

I believe that Terrence always knew that I was not the kind of woman that he needed in his life and I did not belong in the Church circle, and I told him that numerous times. There were always church stories about the minister and women in the congregation, and the confusion that it led to often-forcing people voluntarily to leave their church home because of sexual indiscretions. I was not raised in the type of church environment where the minister was asked to leave the church because he could not keep his pants zipped, and the sisters could not keep their panties pulled up.

I could never understand why a female would stay in a relationship with a preacher and ignore the adultery and out of wedlock children. This seemed so inhumane and so wrong and not of God. I also could not understand my actions.

My enigma would not go away:
So many things did not add up even though I was involved with Terrence before he got divorced. I never met his wife and had no intentions of every meeting her. I do not think that I could bear to see the pain and hurt in her eyes or live with the fact that I may have played a part in them not reconciling their marital differences.

For many years, I blamed myself for what role I played in his divorce even though it had been initiated before I met him. Terrence was a married man, a pastor, and bishop, a liar, and cheat, and was extremely comfortable in his role. I know my role was equally as guilty. However, I wanted to change but found myself continuously pulled back in by his charm.

Terrence, on the other hand, was no different from the other corrupt preachers but I believe, in my heart, that he had some limits as to whom he would fornication with. I do not believe or have ever heard rumors of his getting sexually involved with any of the women in his congregation. He was more sophisticated than that, he only preyed on women who could advance his ministry, and after all, he knew his congregation had an undying dedication to him and required nothing of him except to be a spiritual father to them, and they happily followed his instructions in his absence.

My mistake with Terrence was letting him into my life and in the end, that entrance almost took my life. After my divorce, my mental state was horrible. Terrence seemed to be just the remedy that I needed because when I met this man, a man of GOD, who was charming, sexy, attentive and uninhibited as to what he wanted and desired of me as a female, I was destined to serve him and stay with him as long as he would have me and I him. After the divorce I had lived for a long time feeling unloved, unwanted and empty because the disaster of the legal battle during the divorce. I found myself, for many years, being thrust into a state of depression and low self-esteem. When I met Terrence, I thought that I needed him and Terrence knew that I would never leave him as long as he was taking care of my spiritual and sexual needs.

He always knew that I was a sensual woman and very selective about who I would let into my life and my bed. He was worse than any drug, he was an addiction to me and I had mixed feelings as to whether I wanted to stay in this relationship regardless of all of the turmoil surrounding it.

I never lied to myself about my feelings and the turmoil surrounding the relationship, and did not believe in practicing being a *"hypocrite"*; either I would love him or stay with him regardless of lies, deceit and rumors, or just leave him and never look back.

Terrence at times exhibited a deep level of kindness and compassion however; I could never understand his rationale for being disrespectful to women whether single or married. This type of thinking and behavior has and still confuses me to this day.

Terrence's sexual behavior with married women at conventions was a risk that he would often take—it was apparent to me that these risks were with the approval of other church officials because they took the same risks. Even though he could not perform the sexual acts and indiscretions without the approval of the married women that were involved him, he should however, had some sense of loyalty to ministers who entrusted him with their congregation.

If I were to walk around in a convention, those women were easily identifiable: Most of them being wives of preachers whose churches he would minister at on a frequent basis, and were willing participants. He was a *sociopath* who did not demonstrate any respect for another man's house, with the help of the woman of the house.

On several occasions he was involved with both the wife and the daughter, whose husband and father obviously knew nothing about this because he was promised a co-pastor's position at the church *(even though he was the pastor of his own church*) if he married the minister's daughter. This offer, he stated *"Is very appealing because it will open more doors for me."* I thought to myself, some doors you do not want to enter because it could be a door of no return.

I knew he would not accept the offer because of his ego, and because he was accustom to a lifestyle with no responsibilities. Terrence was a leader and not a follower…to make this kind of transition would be very difficult for him.

When approached about his indiscretions and involvement with wives of other ministers he could be verbally abusive when denying the allegations. To him, I was demon possessed, and Satan's daughter because of my use of profanity whenever I became angry with him about these adulterous affairs.

Of course, these conversations very rarely took place in person because I agreed to eliminate use of profanity in his presence, even though at times I did. Whenever I used profanity, I would always let him know that I was speaking to the man and not the bishop, and the conversations were always in an email or text message. Frankly speaking, he did not deserve any consideration at this point. He always knew that I was very cognizant of his title as a bishop and would not intentional disrespect the office (although we both did because of our sinful relationship).

Surprisingly, he was a quiet man and wanted to stay mostly to himself. He never enjoyed a crowd of people when it did not have anything to do with church and ministering to the congregation, counseling a large group of people, or involved with any type of athletic activity involving golfing and basketball. I always knew he loved God but I just think he was truly demon possessed with a spirit of lust and deception. I knew of the lust because I possessed the exact demon.

Terrence's ruses were more than enough to deceive any unsuspecting female, especially the female wearing his ring.

For six months following the incident in New Jersey, I worked long hours in an attempt to free my mind of this man; even though we both had not resolved the fact that this relationship could not continue.

There were still weekly emails and weekly phone sex when he was not in the city or whenever I did not have the time to travel to the city or state in which he ministered. Over a period during the relationship, I became heartless and cold when it came to sex with him. Foreplay did not matter anymore to me and neither did the cuddling, and words of affection. I did not care if he lied that he desired me for sex; I knew with him, it was just a way of getting laid with a familiar body without having to work for it with someone else. I too, began to feel the same way. We had become mostly sex partners with no strings attached.

I have always felt that this relationship with him would end and the ending would not be a good one.

My concern was not that he had chosen the woman or any other woman for marriage because I never wanted or considered the idea of marriage to him. I was more disturbed that he consistently lied and betrayed me. I had been married; one marriage in my lifetime was enough for me, and my plans for retirement at an early age did not fit into the framework of a life-changing career as the wife of a preacher or anyone else.

I would often tell him that I was not the woman for him because he needed someone subservient that would allow him to do and say, anything he wanted to her—a woman who would remain meek, dutiful and faithful. I on the other hand, if pushed to the limit of no return because of the deceit and lies would not attempt to hurt him in anyway or begrudge him, but all bets are off ... my exit from his life would not have a return date, ever.

Well, I almost did until I was convinced to share my story with the world with hopes to spare thousands the pain of deception by the hustle and seduction in some religious settings.

I knew a day would come when I would have to leave him, to disappear in attempt to get him out of my spirit, to detox from him. He was my addiction and I wanted healing.

I also believe that I too, was the conversation of a pillow talk with one of his other concubines, especially as the sex world refers to it "the bottom Whore," or one of his many thought to be bottom Whorers and Madam.

CHAPTER 9

CHURCH CONVENTION-
The ENTERTAINMENT OF CHOICE

Many of the years during our relationship, I had always joined Bishop Terrence at church conventions at least four times each year. This was our time for bonding in an attempt to clarify our relationship while at the same time completing business deals. The month of September was here and I could not wait to meet him at the convention in Chicago.

He emailed me the dates and location and promised me that this convention would be different for me because he had finally realized that he wanted only me, and he would prove it in his actions if I would only agree to attend. I wanted to believe him because he had made every effort to deny what had been revealed to me in church in New Jersey regarding the female wearing his ring. Since that night, he never missed an opportunity to try to convince me that it was all lies in an attempt to ruin his ministry.

I wanted to believe him because I know that church folks can be just as cruel and hateful as anyone else can — some hide behind the word religion (*as a mantle for moral character*) but inwardly are demonic. The last email he wrote to me prior to my boarding the plane for the convention was a promise to clear up any misunderstandings about his relationship with anyone other than me. Somehow, I knew it was a set-up and he wanted something from me, and that something had to do with me attending the convention. At that point, I did not care because I was getting a vacation away from a very busy life.

I knew that the convention would be quite interesting because the month of September is a very busy month for 2nd ladies and madams. This time of year most preachers dedicated time to them because the 1st lady is usually somewhere visiting for an end of summer vacation. On the other hand, taking advantage of bargains at name brand stores because of the change in season to upgrade their wardrobe for the winter conventions.

I believe that when a person is involved with a married minister, who is a liar, and cheat and is extremely comfortable in his role and believes that he can do no wrong, the fault lies equally between them. I know my role was equally as guilty when it came to Terrence. However, even though I wanted to change, my desire for him prevented my ability to walk out of his life.

To his advantage, he knew I loved him unconditionally…being cognizant of this was more advantageous to him because it was the hook that he held in my soul. He would premeasure my reactions to his indiscretions with other women, and with precision, always had calculated responses to my tantrums even timely purchasing guilt-gifts that he'd used to make up with me.

During many of the conventions the older women in the church (the real financiers of the ministry), would attend every service and seminar that was offered at the convention. They would sit in the services (as if with blinders on that are placed on horses to keep them contained) and praise the corrupt preachers (who are too afraid to grow old), in spite of the knowledge that the preacher fathered many children with inside congregants. Many live vicariously through these ministers and any relationships that they may have… some remain loyal despite paternity scandals, and the displacement of the wife of many years to marry a very younger, vibrant female in the church. In addition, demand the congregation to call her "First Lady." Many insist on the audience to stand up when she enters or is acknowledged before the congregation; not to mention, congregants are expected to give a thunderous applause as if clapping for a superstar... such lunacy. When it is merely his attempt to validate his sin. It doesn't change the fact that she was the other woman while married and hasn't earned the respect of the congregation no matter how he feels about her... which he is entitled to behold, but to inflict the strain on the CREATOR'S house, is an overkill. Moreover, many church mothers help him uphold this errant sociopathic behavior by what they consider is nurturing because they stand by him.

These church mothers are just that, the *surrogate* mother of the church whose duty and obligation is that of admonishing all of their *spiritua*l children of the congregation, including the preacher. The church mothers have to realize that they have some accountability to the congregation when they accept this auxiliary position—it is not an OFFICE of authority according to the Scriptures, but allowed by the pastor to supplement spiritual development.

Some older women are the biggest darn hypocrites—they have a tendency to endorse the acts of the preacher (to many older lonely women, he is their black god), and possibly a secret fantasy. But will indiscriminately use what influence and authority they hold to reprimand and sometimes openly shame the women for their adultery, and fornication with the same preacher. I have seen this many times and it is heartbreaking how the mothers of the church exempt themselves by displaying such piousness.

Although being much older, these women are "church

"CHURCH GIRLS" the Seduction of Religion

girls" too. Many of them function like *MADAMS* and view the male preacher's ability to have multiple relationships a non-issue, by providing cover. These church girls (MOMS) unconsciously have sold their souls just to have that covenant seat on the first row adjacent or right in front of the pulpit. Too often the spiritual tone in the church is ignored...and too much attention and glowing remarks assigned to the "WHORE" they call man of god; A.K.A. "Pastor."

The nice hats and outfits on Sunday and at conventions don't qualify or make a woman a church mother!

See Terrence was surrounded by Church mothers; he was provided this kind of covering that I believe enabled him to frolic with multiple women at conventions; he knew he had their loyalty, which meant he had their money and that afforded him the lifestyle to do what he wanted. To them, he is the greatest orator and most anointed preacher God ever placed on the earth. That is to them.

On occasions, I have had opportunity to be in their presence and faced severe judgment and gossip. I would not dare to speak of his indiscretions for fear that I would be damned; I use to believe these women were such God-fearing saints but in retrospect, realize they had bad attitudes and were co-conspirators in his mess, dressed in their holy white attire and some spoke in tongue.

I knew some of them would be at the convention this year, accompanied by their unmarried daughters, and I would make every effort to avoid them and to stay away from the seminars and many of the other activities. Terrence had revealed to me that several of them had plans for him to become their son-in-law, and I apparently had been an obstacle as to how long it would take the plan to be realized.

They looked upon me as a threat to his ministry, and that he needed to be protected from me. Their perception of the relationship was wrong; I was the one needing the protection.

This particular year was no extraordinary year from any other year. The seating arrangement for the officials of each church, including bishops, evangelists and participants are always up front of the church or auditorium in which the services were held.

Following the evening services the ministers would congregate in one of the other minister's suite, and have a winding down hour or two, before they would venture to their individual rooms.

During this particular year, I was invited to come to the minister's suite for the social hour and dinner. I had never been invited before. I guess one could refer to this as an honor because of the opportunity to be in the presence of such anointed men and women of God.

Terrence knew that I was not the kind of person that cared much about socializing with ministers, but for him I would attend just to show support.

Before I decided to join the others, I returned to my room to freshen up and prepare myself mentally for the many mindless conversations that I had to pretend to be interested in. I was not a socialite unless it was for a meaningful purpose, namely business, and not pleasure.

When I finally arrived at the suite, after an hour of trying to come up with a reason not to attend, I felt somewhat uncomfortable being there. I was not an ordained minister, bible scholar, or an evangelist and I really felt out of place.

The social gala was held in a suite on the 8th floor of the hotel. Most of the convention participants were guests at the hotel and appeared to be very relaxed in this type of environment.

My first observation was that the majority of the guests were the same ministers and bishops who were sitting on the podium during tonight's service. Further observation revealed that the other invited guests included ladies of the evening, (prostitutes). These guests were easily identifiable because they were dressed for the occasion.

I thought to myself, there is not one 1st lady in this crowd. As I began to move through the crowded room, it was obvious that most of the men had decided whom their partner would be for the evening and after the evening events were over.

I thought to myself, what type of convention is this?

"I am over here," I heard Terrence call from the far corner of the room. He was leaning against the wall in deep conversation with several other ministers. As I began to make my way to where he was standing, I felt a light touch on my shoulder. It was Bishop Clayton. "Hi Bishop Clayton," I said. "How are you my dear?" he responded. Bishop Clayton was one of the oldest ministers at the convention and an anointed and dynamite speaker.

"Are you sure you are okay?" he said. "Fine," I said. "Did you enjoy service tonight?"

"Yes sir, I did and I cannot wait until tomorrow," I responded.

We continued in small talk for a few minutes and he seemed so elated to pull out pictures from his wallet to show me his grandchildren. He was such a charming man and seemingly proud of his grandchildren because he spoke of them with such pride and love.

I wondered how and why he was mixed up in this crowd because he was such a sweet man, I thought.

Engrossed in the conversation with Bishop Clayton, I had not noticed that Terrence was now standing next to me to join us in the conversation.

"Hi young man," Bishop Clayton said. "Hi Bishop" Terrence replied. Terrence leaned over and kissed me on the forehead as he had done many times in the past. He had such a way of showing his endearment toward me in a crowd of people, especially when he did not feel threatened about the men in my presence.

The older man smiled and shook Terrence's hand. "That was a great message you delivered tonight young man—I am thinking about how I can persuade you to come to my church on my next church anniversary," Bishop Clayton said. The two men engaged themselves in conversation and I stood there pretending to listen. During their conversation, I found myself becoming more interested in my surroundings than the small talk.

I could easily see why first ladies and other members of these ministers' congregation would not be invited to the after church function. This after party appeared to be more of a *Whorers' convention rather than a Godly church convention.*

I began to sink deeper and deeper into my thoughts and desperately trying so hard to rationalize what I was seeing and experiencing. These ministers obviously were endorsing each other's behavior and none seemed to think it out of the ordinary.

"Bernadette, did you hear what I said?" Terrence asked. "What?" I replied. "Bishop Clayton was asking you about the expansion of his church and the building of a facility for the elderly," Terrence said. "I am sorry but I did not hear you because the music is so loud," I said. I then turned to the Bishop and answered the question he had asked me.

"Young man you have a fine young lady standing next to you and it appears she is not married," the Bishop said. The bishop then grabbed both of my hands and looked at them as if he was examining them. "I see you are not married," he stated. "No," I said, "I am divorced."

"That is no way to live, don't you miss lying in bed at night with someone there to keep you warm?" Bishop Clayton chuckled. I smiled at the old man and out of respect responded, "You are too much bishop and to answer your question I use an electric blanket at night to keep me warm."

Bishop Clayton then turned to Terrence. "I think you need to make an honest woman out of this one because she is definitely a keeper," he stated.

Terrence, having loosen his grip from around my waist, even though I had not noticed that he had placed both of his arms around my waist and was leaning his head on my shoulder, smiled at the bishop. "Are you crazy, do you think I would marry an attorney? She would take me to the cleaners if we got a divorce," he said.

We all laughed. Darn right, I said to myself, plus I would rather die and go to hell before I would commit to becoming a legal servant of your cheating behind, plus I do not like hats and long loose fitting clothing that are purposefully designed for 1st ladies.

I asked both of them to excuse me because I wanted to get something cool to drink. This was my way escaping and making it back to my room before I suffocated.

The room had become crowded, and reeked of stale tobacco, alcohol, perfume, cologne and cheap hooker's hair spray.

The music was loud, and most of the ministers had congregated to the middle of the room—the entertainment tonight was a couple of strippers dressed up in sheer fabrics that revealed their nakedness.

Before I could find the exit, Evangelist Velma who was locked *arm-and-arm* with minister Filbert, stopped me.

I stood there with them for a few minutes and exchanged mindless chitchat with them. Evangelist Velma appeared to be intoxicated and minister Filbert was definitely

"CHURCH GIRLS" the Seduction of Religion

intoxicated because they both stunk of alcohol. He reached over to give me a hug and his hand landed on my breast. "Excuse me," he said. I smiled and said "no harm done." Evangelist Velma gave minister Filbert a tap on the chest, and he reached over to her and placed both of his hands around her lovingly.

I excused myself and headed for the door with them right behind me. It was obvious that they were headed in the same direction when they left the social gathering.

When I got to the doorway to enter into the hallway I was again approached but this time by one of the musicians that played for Terrence. "Ms. Davis, the bishop asked me to let you know that he was going to his room to get some rest and would see you tomorrow," the musician said. I thanked him and proceeded to my room.

This was very odd and out of the ordinary because it had never happened before, I thought to myself. Had I been dumped for a Madam? Very interesting. I went to my room and slept peacefully that night. I really believed Terrence wanted to rest so I did not attempt to contact him until the next morning.

Around 11 am, I decided to go into the hotel restaurant and enjoy a late morning breakfast. This was after I tried calling Terrence around 10 am; I had made an effort to contact him and ask him to join me for breakfast. There was no answer when I telephoned him so I decided I would just eat alone. I knew that Terrence would be involved in a seminar at 1:00pm and he probably was preparing for that. He has always taken his teaching serious. So I didn't think too about not reaching him by telephone.

When I unlocked my door and entered the hotel hallway, it was empty and there was no sign of life anywhere.

I thought to myself, everyone must be involved in the seminars because the registration was quite expensive for this convention.

I walked to the elevator and stood there waiting for it to come to the 5th floor so I could go down and eat. I was so hungry and felt that I had not eaten in a month. The elevator door finally opened and I stepped in not paying any attention to the people who had gotten on before me. I pushed the button for the lobby floor before I turned my attention to the other elevator guests.

To my surprise, there in the far right corner of the elevator stood Terrence and Evangelist Blackman standing so close one could barely tell where his arm ended and hers began.

In his baritone voice he was speaking such loving words, and finding it exciting, she began to giggle. They were so entrenched in the conversation that Terrence never noticed that I was on the elevator.

The elevator stopped on the 4th floor and I had to move over so some of the guests could exist. I made sure that I positioned myself close enough to Terrence so that he could feel and see my presence. "Good Morning Bishop Terrence, how are you this morning? I hope you slept well," I said. They both spoke and he never acknowledged that he knew me.

I stood staring at the elevator door and could not wait until it landed at the lobby level. Before I made it to the lobby, the elevator stopped at another floor.

I stood frozen as the door opened for the 3rd floor. Terrence and Evangelist Blackman moved to the front of the elevator and proceeded to exit. Before he made his exist, he casually glanced in my direction. At that point, my dignity told me to push the lobby button, but my mind said to get out of the elevator and slap the taste out of his mouth. I chose my mind.

I walked off the elevator and called out to him four times before he turned to acknowledge me. I began to walk toward him with such anger and venom that I am sure my skin color had changed right before his eyes.

"Terrence I know you are not making an attempt to disrespect me by not acknowledging me, are you?" I said. "I know you recognized me in the elevator and it was obvious you were attempting to ignore, right!" I said.

Terrence finally turned around, but before he did, he said something to Evangelist Blackman who thought that the comment was funny. He hurriedly tried to reach my side because he knew there was about to be a nasty unveiling in the hallway. I stood near the elevator and waited for him to approach me. He appeared to be as angry as I was but I was refusing to step down this time. "You will never change and you are a disgusting human being," I said.

At that point, I heard him say something to me but by that time, it was too late because I had raised my arm and slapped him across his face.

The next thing I knew Terrence had forcefully jammed me up against the elevator trying to calm me down and talk to me. "Bernadette, let's go to your room right now," he said. I twisted free of him and attempted to gain some sense of control. We stood there in silence for a few minutes and he was trying to explain some meaningless lies that I did not want to hear.

The entire time he was standing near me trying to explain his actions, I noticed the female carefully approaching us to observe the outcome of the scene that had just taken place in the hotel hallway. "Miss," I said, "I would stay out of this because you see, it is what one would refer to as a lover's argument between a female and a lying, cheating, deceitful and good for nothing anointed man of God."

I did not realize that Terrence was still holding my hand; eventually I pulled my hand free and headed down the hallway to the exit leading to the lobby. I had not noticed that during this entire disturbance we had company in the hallway. I got a glimpse of three men standing near Terrence, who had obviously approached him as I was walking away. I recognized one of the men and Bishop Clayton. It was Bishop Clayton that said, "Young man you were wrong in your actions. That young lady does not deserve to be humiliated here at this convention or anywhere else."

Tell him bishop, I thought. You also know that he is a no good for nothing shell of a man. The scene devastated me because I just could not believe that he would invite another

"CHURCH GIRLS" the Seduction of Religion

one of his concubines to the convention, after lying to me about why he wanted me to attend this convention. I could have stayed home and not be traumatized like this, but he didn't care.

I entered the restaurant, ate a healthy breakfast, and read the newspaper. I had finally calmed down from the excitement on the 3rd floor. Once again, I thought, he had helped me to display foolishness in public.

After I finished breakfast, I headed back to my room on the 5th floor and decided to pack and leave the convention and never look back. I could not understand why Terrence would invite me and then disrespect me. I knew that I would be the gossip topic for the after church social event tonight but I could care less because they were all hypocrites, except Bishop Clayton, I thought. He is just an old man.

I took the newspaper back to my room to finish reading it before I decided to pack and book a flight. I had decided to go to Los Angeles to visit my brother and his wife who I had not seen for four years.

I laid across the bed and began to assess my actions. I rolled over and started laughing aloud. The look on Terrence's face gave me joy. Once again, he was found out.

In the "old days," my actions would have been referred to as "stupid." While in this day and age, I referred to it as the angry sinful madam who did not get the privilege of providing service to the preacher at the convention, because the *"anointed one"* decided to choose a more suitable partner for the night; the highly anointed *evangelist* concubine. The thought of this assessment made me laugh even harder. I had finally gone insane.

That night, when I was supposed to be in church, I made reservations to travel to California. The visit was long overdue and a vacation was what I needed being that I had taken two weeks off to travel with Terrence in an attempt to save our relationship. Now was the right time to seek out rest and relaxation so I could gather my thoughts and work toward rebuilding my life, and returning to the person who once had ethics, morals and values. The past years since I met this preacher I had lost all of my integrity.

I could not once again defy the house of God, and run behind Terrence who had already assisted me voluntarily in destroying my relationship with God. At this juncture, only my faith and remembrance of my past fellowship with God and his son Jesus Christ is the sustaining force in my life.

I had felt completely void before today and following the confrontation with Terrence, the emptiness subsided after finding new strength to move forward. Everyone should only be willing to sink so low in the name of love, and I had had enough of this nonsense. Someone has to be praying for me, I thought.

My flight would not be leaving until 1:00pm the following day so I had the opportunity to get a good night sleep and take my time packing. I ordered room service so I could continue to relax and gather myself. Before I ate, I ran the bathtub full of hot water and poured in some relaxing ingredients to sooth me. I needed to rest as well as a quiet and peaceful night.

I turned on a movie, crawled into bed, and placed my evening meal in the center of the bed. This is heavenly, I thought.

After I finished my meal, I went into the bathroom, to brush and floss my teeth. From a glimpse in the mirror, I noticed that I was looking tired these days and my energy was at its lowest.

I felt that I had aged 20 years since I had become in involved with Terrence. Initially I believed that the relationship with Terrence would put some "pep back in my step," but instead it was slowly killing me. My divorce did not do me this bad.

I made it back to the bed and crawled under the covers.

I turned the television up to drown out any noise that would be coming from the 5th floor hallway when all of the church folks decided to go back to their rooms for the evening.

Around twelve midnight I was awaken out of my sleep because I felt a draft coming from my room door. I sat up in bed and there standing in the doorway was Terrence. I had forgotten that he had a key to my room and it was obvious I had not put on the night security latch.

I sat there staring at him as he closed the door. "I am sorry that I disturbed you, go back to sleep. I just came to check on you and make sure you are okay," he said.

I laid back down on the bed and covered my body and made myself comfortable again so I could go back to sleep. I thought to myself, this must be a dream because he has to be a fool to come into this room. Doesn't he know I am a deranged woman?

I closed my eyes in hopes of falling back into a deep sleep. He knew that all of his options of ever making a fool out of me were gone.

I knew that he had cast me aside because I had already heard through the grapevine of gossip that he had become involved with another female attorney out of Texas, and a medical internist. He was moving up on the ladder, I wish him well. Good for him.

After I laid down, I had not thought of whether he was lingering around in the room stalking me or whether he had gone shortly into the night. He was a very intelligent man, and I am sure he figured it out that I was done with him.

If the Holy Spirit had not revealed that to him, I am sure my silence did. He should have gotten the message that I did not care anymore and I was not going to let him drag me further into hell or, participate in another opportunity to perform a jealous demonic ritual in front of these church people. The room was silent and I decided to drift back off to sleep.

No sooner than I drifted back off to sleep, I was awaken again by Terrence. He had crawled into bed with me and I could feel his naked body pressing up against mine. "Terrence why don't you go back to your room or choose a concubine to service you tonight as you did last night," I said. "I am just not in the mood for this tonight and as a matter of fact no night in the future," I said. He was silent.

We both laid there in silence for an hour with his arms around my waist and his warm naked body pressing against my back, buttocks and thighs. It felt right and I could feel myself being absorbed into him. Loving Terrence kept me confused and stressed. I drifted back off to sleep.

It wasn't long before I was awaken again when Terrence broke the silence in the room by reaching over me and turned on the radio, which was on the nightstand. "The old Mack daddy move," I thought. He knew that music would calm both of us down. We often listened to music after he preached. He was into Jazz and I was into any music he enjoyed.

"I see your bags are almost packed; where are you traveling to tomorrow?" he asked softly. "I think California," I said. "What part of California?" he asked. "Just California," I replied. He knew that I had the ability to disappear without a trace from his sorry self and when I decided it to be officially over between us there was no going back. There was one thing this relationship had taught me, Terrence was not capable of being in a monogamous relationship and no one female could satisfy him.

I have always succumb to his touch and his lovemaking. I could never turn him away because I have always enjoyed making love with him, and he is the only man who has ever made me experience more than two orgasms in one night.

Any woman who has ever been involved with Terrence should understand that he is not a one-woman man, and never will be. I have to believe that he did not intend to ever form a permanent relationship with me and nor did I desire such a relationship.

He was not a selfish sex partner and neither was I. With me, Terrence would use whatever sex acts would give me pleasure. I could feel him moving around in the bed and in a split second, he was positioning my body by pulling my hips against him as he knelt down in the middle of the bed. I let myself relax and allowed him to enter me. When we both reached the sexual height of no return, he turned me over on my back and lowered his head onto my stomach and my body exploded.

We made love for several hours. I just did not care about my feelings or care if there was a future for us. I only wanted to be with him in this moment in time. He was making love to me as if this was the last time and he was gentle with my body. In all of the years of making love to him, I had never experienced the feelings that I felt tonight. It was as if we were making love for the first time. I clung to him and did not want to let go. I cannot remember how long he laid there holding me after we both were exhausted from loving each other. He held me as I pressed my face into his chest. We were silent with no words exchanged between us.

I do not remember when he left the room. I only remember waking up at 10:00 in the morning and he was gone.

CHAPTER 10

CAN I BE REDEEMED AND STILL LIVE?

After being in California for two weeks, I decided to extend the time. I called my office and arranged for coverage in my absence. There was no return date in mind. Maybe this should be a permanent transition, I thought.

For the entire time that I was in California, I avoided contact with Terrence. I thought it best because my mental state was fragile and I had lost all decision-making skills when it came to him. It was a difficult time for me and I became a recluse. Weeks turned into two months. Most of my time was spent reading. My brother and his wife traveled often so I had the house to myself. My brother lived in a gated community so it was no problem being in the house alone.

I began to attend church again and familiarize myself with books of the bible in which I had not read in years. I even took the time to talk to God and work on my repentance. After two months, I began to regain clarity about my relationship with God and understood that I was not alone, only blinded by sin. I was seeking after man and not God. In the name of religion, I was seduced and committed seduction.

I asked myself a thousand times, why did I allow this man to blind me to what was right; why was his grip on my soul so binding. When did I lose my strength to walk away? I never was attracted to preachers, and I had to be insane.

I tried to make the best of my time away and spent most of the days in the backyard sitting in the gazebo reading or walking through flea markets. I took long walks in hopes of regaining my strength and energy. It was so apparent to me that I was often tired and exhausted without any cause or reason. I was mentally drained.

One day while lying around reading, I suddenly began to experience sharp pain in my lower abdomen. I knew I could not be pregnant because all precautions had been taken to avoid ever bringing a child into this world again. I had love for my one and ONLY child, and was selfish to the point that I did not have time for any one particular project, and especially one that would include raising another child. Sex to me, was for pleasure only and not for bringing another child into this world that I had to be responsible for. My actions had been irresponsible on my part, so why could I not be pregnant and carrying this man's child. "No baby-in-baby carriage" — being bound to a man, especially, a wondering one like Terrance, was not in my future. Not once had I thought of cancer or any other disease that could cause such pain.

I decided to contact a physician's office in the area and get a complete medical checkup. I realized that I had not had a yearly physical for the past three years and one was overdue. I also decided that I would get tested for communicable diseases even though there were no signs of any type of sexual disease, but knowing of his sexual habits, it was now high on the list, even though we had been careful at the end of the relationship. However, *"How careful were you throughout the relationship?" I said to myself.*

A week following my physical exam and a series of blood work and examinations in hopes of identifying the cause of my abdominal pain, I was notified to come into the doctor's office for the results. Nervous and upset, I became panicky and in dire need of support and comfort. I felt that Terrence was the only one who could quiet my fears if he would only make time in his busy schedule to be here with me for comfort and support. But would he if I had asked him. Having such uncertainty about him was not conducive to my fragile state-of-mind.

After a few minutes, I ruled against the idea because I knew he would never come. He was not that type of person who would care what happened to one of his concubines.

Circumstances have a way of deceiving a person when one is faced with an urgent and perhaps critical medical situation that could transform their life. I felt that I was in that place and needed him to be with me.

That thought slowly dissipated when I thought of the last day that I met him. It was painfully clear I was only another female he pursued and conquered, and another topic of conversation. He never loved me.

I entered the doctor's office and sat for what appeared to be an eternity. When the nurse came to escort me into the doctor's office, I had been sitting in the waiting room for almost an hour staring into space and out of contact with reality. While sitting there I only heard about ten minutes of the conversations going on between the other patients waiting to be seen by the doctor. I never meant to be unapproachable by not socializing with the other ten people in the room; I just wanted to see the doctor, get the horrible news and crawl up somewhere and die. I had become very depressed and felt like a recluse and no one was going to change that.

When I came out of my trance, and got passed feeling sorry for myself, I realized that I was sitting next to a woman who appeared to be around the age of seventy. I pretended to ignore her mere existence and reached over to the table that was separating our seating arrangement, and carefully selected a magazine to glance through while I was waiting for my medical results. I tried to read but could sense the woman sitting there staring at me; it was apparent there was no getting out of talking to this one.

She is just going to force a conversation on me. I decided to cooperate with what was bound to happen. I looked over at her and smiled.

We began to make small talk about the office decorations among other things, when she began to breathe hard.

"Are you okay?" I asked. "Fine," she said. "I just need to finish here so that I can get something to eat." She laid her head back on the chair and closed her eyes.

"At my age it has always been amazing to me how God has always had his hands on my life; chose me from birth, anointed me during my childhood, and carried me through all of the problems in my life. Including all of my pain and sorrows, two divorces, and in the present dilemma. I have always tried to be obedient but I sit here waiting for a prognosis of an illness that invaded my body and only God knows how long it has been lingering.

I looked at the woman with concern and reached over to touch her hand. At that time, the nurse beckoned me to come in to see the physician. I began to sweat and breathe hard. I felt as if I was drowning. "It is alright dear," all the time I was sitting with her, she said, "I was praying for both of us." God wanted me to share that story with you, you see, I have been diagnosed with breast cancer. She reached into her purse and handed me a card, she was an evangelist from Texas. I agreed to attend her church when I was abled and proceeded into the doctor's office.

I sat at the front of the doctor's desk as he began to read over my chart. He studied the results very carefully before looking up at me.

"Ms. Davis," he said, *"The result of your exam shows that you have a tubular pregnancy and is in need of surgery."*

"Have you been bleeding?"

"Hemorrhaging" I said, *"for the past two weeks and then it stopped. I thought that I was bleeding extra hard because I have not been feeling well these days."*

What a life changing experience, an experience that could have caused me to lose my life if it had not been for the grace of God. How could I have been so careless?

The doctor explained the side effects of the tubular pregnancy and suggested that I go into surgery immediately. I informed him that I lived miles away from the hospital with my brother and his wife, and had been visiting for only three months. "Doctor, is it safe to travel back to Pennsylvania and go into the hospital for this procedure?" I asked. "No, you have to have surgery immediately. I suggest you stay in the hospital now and be admitted. The surgery can be scheduled for tomorrow," he said. I knew it would be futile to contest… I decided to come back the next day because I didn't want to stay overnight. "Thank you doctor," I said.

"CHURCH GIRLS" the Seduction of Religion

I walked out of the doctor's office and looked around for the woman that shared her life story with me. I don't know why I felt the urge to hug her and thank her for talking and being so nice to me. I glanced toward the door leading to the examination rooms and saw her slowly walking into another exam room. I will see her later, perhaps at a church service.

I did not feel the impact of the news nor felt depressed about the diagnosis I had received. The doctor had made all of the arrangements for surgery, and scheduled the procedure for the next day.

I was not aware of what the doctor's diagnosis would be when I got to his office so I rented a car and booked myself a hotel room near his office before coming in to see him.

Although I am an independent grown up who did not feel so grown up at this time, chose it this way because I did not want my brother or my parents to worry about me.

I made it back to my room after stopping to get something to eat. I sat in a restaurant alone and thought about how I would adjust and what I should do after the surgery. I was too tried to take a bath and take off my clothes so I took off my shoes, and laid across the bed.

I lay there on the bed thinking about what I would do with my life while slowly massaging my abdomen. If it had been different, I thought, I would have put aside being selfish and raised this child on my own. I would not have let Terrence know of this pregnancy and just disappeared forever, maybe travel back to Texas and work with the immigrants.

I drifted off to sleep for a few minutes because I knew that I had to check out of the hotel. It was early and I had time to check out and be at the hospital by 7pm, which was the time that the doctor had scheduled for me to be admitted. "This will give the hospital staff enough time to get all blood work and prep you for surgery," he said.

I always stayed at motels when I had to travel out of the city with the Terrence. He would often tease me about choosing motels on the other side of the city, and as far away from him as I could get when I was traveling with him. Motel rooms verses hotel rooms gave me a sense of privacy. To me it was disrespectful for me to stay in the same hotel as Terrence, even if I visited him during the night I would slept in my own bed and in my own room after we made love. Terrence put up a fuss at the beginning of our relationship because I chose not to stay in the same hotel but found himself agreeing with me, especially because the host minister always wanted to drive him back to his hotel and sit awhile-discussing business after service.

In my paranoid jealous state of mind, I also believe that Terrence, more than likely, was dating someone from the church and had midnight visits by someone else other than me when I was not traveling with him.

A woman in every port, I thought, he should have been a sailor because he sure had the characteristics of one; if it was true that sailors had a woman in every port.

Lying flat on the bed was uncomfortable so I decided to sit up in a chair and put my feet up on the bed. When I tried to pull myself up from the bed, I felt sharp pains penetrating my lower body. The pain was so excruciating and I found myself crying out. Must be the food I ate, I thought. I felt an urge to use the bathroom. Perhaps that would help, I thought.

When I finally stood up, I experienced a sharp pain shoot through the lowest part of my abdomen. I did not want to believe that I would have my baby right here in the motel room, but it was a possibility. I reached over in my purse to locate my cell phone so I could call an ambulance. I gave the information to the 911 operator. In an attempt to make it to the bathroom I again tried to stand and passed out on the floor.

When the ambulance got to the room, I was lying in a pool of blood holding my abdomen. The warm fluid flowing from beneath my lower garment was continuing to trickle down.

The ambulance took me to the hospital and I was admitted through the emergency room. After the doctor examined me, I was taken immediately into surgery. "Ms. Davis," the doctor said, "we have to perform a hysterectomy; I am sorry, you lost the baby and you are hemorrhaging and losing a lot of blood. We have to get you into surgery now because it cannot wait until morning."

The blood was flowing down profusely.

I signed consent forms for the surgery and provided whatever information was required. Not once did I get panicky because I knew that for some reason, I was not alone and everything was going to work out for me. I had my future ahead of me and I was not dying of some incurable disease, not at this time.

The anesthesiologist completed his prep for surgery and I was taken in by stretcher into the surgery room. The doctor came in and asked "is there family outside we need to speak to after surgery?"

"No." I knew I had to face my punishment alone. Death of my child and a hysterectomy and no one has knowledge of this except the medical personnel.

A secret I will have to live with for the rest of my life and pain of the loss of a child that will haunt me to my grave.

I was taken from surgery to the intensive care unit. There obviously had been some complications during the surgery; I lost a lot of blood and was later informed that my bladder had ruptured.

When I awoke, tubes and monitors surrounded me. It appeared to me that the death angel had visited me, but God allowed me to live a little longer.

Disoriented and confused, I remembered feeling that I was thirsty and wanted a drink of water. In an attempt to get up to get water, my movements caused the monitors to beep. I just wanted to go home.

My body hurt all over and there was not one part of my body that did not hurt.

The nurse placed a wet cloth to my lips, and after being administered more pain medication, I fell asleep. I was later told that the doctor ordered that I remained medicated because of the surgical complications, which had been life threatening.

My body temperature had reached 104 degrees, my bladder had ruptured, and my appendix had to be removed. Of all things, my appendix had ruptured prior to me being admitted to the hospital.

When I finally was able to sit up in the bed after three days of being highly medicated. It was apparent that the nurses had been taking excellent care of me. Most of the monitors had been removed and there only remained three drainage tubes in place. I felt strong enough to sit up in bed and was able to observe the surgical scars.

The tubular pregnancy had created medical problems, which resulted in a total hysterectomy. After three days of being in the intensive care unit, I was finally moved to a private room away from all of the monitors and life support machines, but the tubes remained intact.

The tenth day following the surgery, I would finally be discharged.

As I lay in the bed, I had to decide what I would do next. Would I go back home to the lonely house or would I travel and go into seclusion until I could find the strength to transition back into society.

Around 2pm of my discharge, the doctor and nurse came into my room and gave post-surgical discharge instructions. I thanked everybody and was transported down to the lobby where a taxi was waiting for me. The rental car company had been given instructions to pick up the rental car that I had driven so that would not be a problem. I had the taxi to drop me off at a nearby motel where I would be near the hospital for my checkup visit in five days.

The days and nights were difficult for me and I was unable to sleep. I became hot one second and cold the next. The doctor had written a prescription for estrogen and a strong pain medication but I had tossed it in the trash on the way out. I refused to take medicine, pain medicine or otherwise. I was determined.

In five days, I arrived at my follow-up appointment and informed the doctor of my symptoms as he removed stitches and changed my abdominal wound dressings. My body looked like a road map with all of the stitches.

The doctor suggested that I participate in a therapy group for women who had undergone a hysterectomy and the loss of a child. I refused, and thanked him because I knew that this was between God and me; I was being punished for my involvement with Terrence and my acts of defiance inside of God's house.

I hired the taxi to take me back to the motel so I could rest and plan out my next strategy. I had contacted my family and they all thought that I had taken a vacation and was having fun. It was normal for me to get in my car, drive, and end up anywhere. I enjoyed driving and relishing the scenery and concentration. I did not believe in driving with a radio blasting or any type of noise, just peace and quiet, and that is just what I had planned on doing once I reached my destination.

I laid around for several days and decided to take a flight to El Paso, Texas because I did not know anyone there but had recalled the wonderful scenery, and the quietness of the area while traveling across country with my son and ex-husband.

My body began to heal and I was feeling better each day.

A week later, after being in El Paso, I decided to rent a car and drive back to California. The trip was longer than I had anticipated and it took me three days to arrive at the California state line. During the three days, I took my time driving and stopping at roadside shops to collect gifts to send home to my parents. They loved rare items so I was selective in what I chose.

When I entered California, I checked into the nearest hotel. The next day I decided that I would drive to San Diego and then go across the Mexican border to purchase cowboy boots, some of the leather belts and pouches. I wore cowboy boots most of the year except the summer.

When I reached San Diego, I checked into a hotel, took a long shower, and fell fast asleep. The long drive had taken a toll, and was tiring; I realized that I was not as strong as I thought following the surgery.

When I woke up the next morning, I felt something warm flowing from my vagina. I was hemorrhaging. I was surprised that I had no pain. I washed up and drove to the nearest hospital. I was admitted into the hospital for three days. Post-surgical tissue had been torn and separated and required a new cut and stitching in the lower abdominal part of my body.

After being released, I decided to stay in San Diego for a few weeks and pamper myself. I needed to heal both physically and mentally. It was apparent that I had been exerting too much pressure on my body and had not given my body ample time to heal. I had trouble facing the fact that my body needed time to heal.

Probably more time than it would take for my mental state and emotions to heal.

I sat around the hotel room and read a lot. Reading gave me comfort, and healing for the soul. Not one time did I consider picking up the phone to contact Terrence. After surgery, I had changed my cell phone number and no one except my family was able to contact me. I wanted to be left in peace.

CHAPTER 11

IS IT FINALLY OVER?

After two weeks of being in San Diego, I decided to go through my telephone book; I remembered that I had an old nursing school classmate, Coritha that was in San Diego working on her doctorate degree. So I called to invite her to dinner at the hotel.

When she arrived at my room, we ordered dinner and talked about our younger days. She looked at me and said, "You are not looking well, are you sick?" "No" I said, "I am just having trouble keeping food down. Every time I drink or eat, I throw it back up. It must be a virus or something," I said, and began to weep. For hours, we sat there and I told her what I had gone through. She tried to comfort me by telling me of her woes but it did not help. No one could possibly be suffering like me, I said.

"A lot of people are suffering but in different ways," she replied.

Coritha decided to stay at the hotel with me that night and I felt like I needed someone to be there in case of another emergency. The next morning I felt better but remained in bed for the rest of the day. She left and returned to her apartment and told me to call her if I needed anything.

She was always my best friend in college and one that understood me. It has been too long since I have been in contact with childhood friends; I have to do better.

When you are alone, the days have a way of lingering. The San Diego landscape was so beautiful and the skies clear, everything seemed perfect to me even in my state of mind. I had always loved living in California and was glad that I had returned to recoup and rest.

The weekend came and my friend volunteered to drive me across the Mexican border so we could shop. We spent the day going in and out of shops, trying on boots, belts, and hats. We chose to stay for the night's festivities and had a great time. There were some military families visiting that time of year, one in particular with whom we shared small talk and paired up for the evening, toured several famous streets and tapped in to the night scene for entertainment.

This was refreshing to me and I began to feel like my old self, happy and peaceful. Amazingly, what I had been through the last several months of my life was such a distant matter. At this very moment, it did not matter. I felt at peace.

We made it back across the border around midnight and traveled back to the hotel.

The next day we visited the beach and I laid in the sun and slept right on the sand. My girlfriend invited her fiancé, who was also attending the same university. He decided to bring along a friend of his, which resulted in disaster. I was cordial but not in the friendly mood. She must have shared with them that I was not feeling well and they seem to understand my behavior. We went to dinner; I could not eat because my stomach was still not ready to receive food. The entire day was nice and the company was welcomed.

After they dropped me back at the hotel, I took a bath and immediately went to bed. When I entered the room, the darkness was surrounding me and I began to feel lonely again.

To eliminate the loneness, I called my son who was

living in Japan. He landed a job there and was having the time of his life. We always traveled together as a family during my marriage and it was said traveling was in his blood. I was glad that he was in another country because he always was able to sense when something was wrong.

The telephone rang several times before he answered, "Hi mama," he said, "what's wrong?" "Nothing," I said. "I am in California on vacation and I was just thinking about my baby." I then proceeded to tell him about my trip to Mexico. He talked for about thirty minutes and then hung up. I held the phone for a few minutes before I hung up. He was fine and that made me feel better.

The next three days I stayed in bed and only got up to take a bath and use the bathroom. I sipped on fluid, vomited, sipped fluid and vomited. I was determined to get better before I left the state. I began slowly to get better, strong enough to travel.

Some people would refer to my actions as running away from my problems; I referred to my actions of running to a solution to my problems.

I checked the flights to Florida and decided to go and visit my parents for a few days. That would do me good and they would be happy to see me. My father had been ill and the trip was way overdue because I had not seen my parents in two years.

When I arrived in Florida, the weather was very hot. I rented a car and drove to my parents' house. Before I made it to the family farm, I decided to drive by my old college, high school and elementary school. I felt a need to return to my roots, to where I was happy and felt safe.

When I arrived at my parents' house, we greeted each other, sat, and talked for hours. My parents could sense something was wrong with me but never said a word about it. That night I slept on the sofa and watched television until I fell asleep.

For the seven days of the visit, I helped my parents attend the garden, feed the chickens, slop the hogs, feed the horses and collect eggs from the chickens.

The night before I left, we attended bible study and I was among family and friends. I felt nothing or no one could hurt me there. I did not want to leave but I knew that I had to resolve several unfinished issues in my life. I knew I could not hide here forever. I had to face my life and deal with my problems.

I kissed both of my parents goodbye and as always, they both gave me money. I did not need the money but accepted it anyways. This gift of money meant more to them than to me because they always thought they should take care of their children financially, no matter how educated or old the children were.

"Buy yourself some clothes," my mama said, "you always did dress different from the other children, and why are your jeans torn and you are wearing that sloppy shirt?" "Also, go get a haircut because I have never seen your hair look like that," daddy said.

Little did they know this was my dress code and I had

worn this short curly hairstyle for the past two years. "I think I look good," I said. Mama smiled and shook her head.

I grabbed my bags and put them into the car to head for the airport. Where to, I said to myself.

When I arrived in Pennsylvania, I became panicky because I had not been home for many months. I felt like a stranger in a foreign land. I did not want to see or speak to anyone until I could figure out what I would do as far as my career, or what was left of it. I knew that I did not want to live here and could not after all that I had experienced. This is where all of my problems began.

I knew that I had to move away from this area and this would be the only solution if I wanted to heal.

Before returning to Pennsylvania, I had been in contact with a real estate agent and put my house on the market for sale. I had been out of the state for almost a year. The return trip to Pennsylvania would last only long enough to close on my house.

Prior to my departure from Pennsylvania, I had asked one of my colleagues to house sit and take care of my puppy, and make sure that the upkeep of the house was livable and appealing to potential buyers.

With thoughts of going to a hotel and not staying at the house, I entered the house and decided that I should pack some clothes. I felt that I could not stay in the house for a single night. I could not lie in the bed where Terrence and I had made love.

My heart and emotions had become void of any feeling.

I just did not care anymore about the words love, trust, friendship or commitment because any mental connections with those feelings did not *exist* in my life anymore.

When I entered my bedroom, I sat on the bed and started to cry uncontrollably. Everywhere I looked were signs of Terrence, his shirts, shaving products, even his hairbrush. I had not released all of the pain and hurt until now. I cried for hours and eventually fell asleep; I did not make it to the hotel that night. The next day I went to closing on my house.

The following day after my closing, I drove to my old office building to see all of my colleagues and associates before departing the next day for Texas. When I entered my office, everyone was happy to see me. Nothing had changed it was business as usual. No one questioned me about why I decided to take a trip for such a long period but was eager to hear about my adventures out west.

I showed pictures of the trip and the beautiful scenery. That night I decided to join some of my office colleagues for dinner and actually enjoyed the evening. I thought it was nice just to be among friends but how long can I put forth this face of happiness, and act as if my life had not changed. My relationship with the bishop had drastically changed my life; I had left behind in Texas my health, and a deceased child that I could not tell him about. I felt that I could not reveal any of the experiences from the past months. Not to Terrence or my family.

After surgery the remains of my deceased son was placed in my hands. I arranged for the remains to be transported to El Paso, Texas, where I buried him. I knew that

I would be moving to El Paso at some point in time and I just wanted my son there so that I could visit his small grave. I prayed that my son had survived for a short period in my tubes but never had a chance at life. I found myself, at times, questioning God.

While in Texas, I had arranged to work with an immigration firm. The firm did not pay much but it would give me pleasure to be able to have the flexible time to go into the office or work at home. I knew that I would enjoy gardening while my puppy run around in the yard chasing flying insects, and I could go shopping at junk stores, garage sales and antique shops.

I was finally in a place in my life where I could begin to heal and find myself again. Even though I was self-sustaining financially, I always had someone to take care of me and to be there for me when the times were hard. I always had companionship and never without it.

The nurturing from my parents, my ex-husband and the preacher had spoiled me. I did not know what it felt like being alone.

The day of departure from Pennsylvania, I went out to a nearby mall to do some shopping. While walking through the mall window-shopping, I heard someone call out my name. When I turned around to see who it was, I came face-to-face with Evangelist White. We began to talk and the woman told me that Terrence was in the city and ministering at her Church. He had been in the city for five days for her pastor's anniversary.

"CHURCH GIRLS" the Seduction of Religion

"I know you will be there" she exclaimed, "Because I know you enjoy his preaching." I smiled at her and agreed to see her there. *I had attended church service at that church on many occasions and at one time, I had considered becoming a member.* The Evangelist was an associate pastor of the church and I had heard her minister. "I will try to be there," I said, and walked away feeling a sense of do I flee or face him.

I stopped in at a coffee shop in the mall and sat down at one of the tables, ordered coffee and made a call to the airlines to reschedule my flight for the next day; I wanted a morning flight to Texas so I could settle in early. A part of me needed to see Terrence. I speculate since he was an integral figure in my life that had not been replaced a part of me did not want to sever all contact and ties with him. I had not been in contact for months and I just needed to see him before I departed.

I stayed out and walked the mall for hours. It felt good shopping for new outfits and shoes. I decided to get my nails done, a facial and a massage. When I arrived home, there was a note on my front door. I opened the note and read it. "Why haven't you been in contact with me? Call me," and left a telephone number.

That was quick I said, no one could keep a secret.

I went into the house and took a nap to rest from shopping. Around 7:30 pm, I got dressed and carefully applied my makeup. I wore a black dress accented with gold accessories. See Terrence made a mistake in telling me that he preferred his women to wear black accented with pearls, so I refused to look like the other concubines that would dress according to his liking. Can you imagine five or more women sitting in close proximity dressed in black wearing pearls? Nope, not wearing the uniform anymore I said.

So I wore my high heels that strapped around my ankle; I needed the support to stand in case by some unforeseen reason I had to steady myself when I walked into the church. I sprayed on my favorite perfume, brushed my curly hair and headed for my car.

The drive to the church was about 45 minutes. This gave me an opportunity to compose myself and think of how I would respond to him if I were cornered. I had to do this and there was no way out of it. I remembered how he tried to reduce my confidence and contain me like a puppet, and now I finally have the chance to let him know that he had not won in his attempt to break me. I was as strong as he was, and a survivor. Although, what he did take from me was the ability to "love another man."

The church was packed as usual. He had not entered the pulpit when I arrived at the church and I was happy about that. I was escorted close to the front of the church where I sat on an outside seat so that if it became too uncomfortable, I could leave when the congregation got happy and stood up.

The choir sang, and the church went through the routine of collections and taking care of church business. I sat next to a female who I represented in a child support dispute. I had taken her on as a client several years prior and she still remembered me. She was very chatty; she talked a lot about the case and how her baby's daddy was still no good, as she referred to him. "That is going around these days," I said.

"Do you have children?" She asked. And without looking in her direction, I said "One child, he is grown and working overseas." She continued to chat and I found myself lost in my thoughts, mostly what time I would leave for my flight the next morning and how long it would take me to find a place to live in Texas.

"Let's stand," the minister of the house said. I looked up and saw Terrence and ten other ministers and pulpit guests enter the pulpit.

When Terrence walked in, he greeted everyone on the pulpit before he took a seat in the middle chair. I felt my knees shaking and had to hold onto the pew in front of me for fear that I would fall. You have to get through this, I said to myself, you have to stay here and say your goodbye to him; you owe that to yourself and to him. Why I considered him, who knows.

Terrence was finally introduced to the congregation after a lengthy discourse of introductions and other church polity. When Terrence took his place behind the podium, the congregation was asked to take their seats.

I found myself staring at him and could not take my eyes off him. All of the feelings that I thought had left me resurfaced. I forgot about the pain, surgery, and all that I had experienced. His voice rang out in a high worship and the congregation went wild. I was mesmerized and found myself lost in the service as the other church members did.

Near the end of the service, the coward in me rose up and I knew that I had to leave before service was over. He had located me and had spent most of the night looking in my direction as he delivered the word for the night.

I did not know what the title of the sermon was and did not care as long as I could hear his voice. I refused to look directly into his eyes, avoided standing most of the night, and thanked God that I could use the congregation members that were sitting in front of me as a shield when they stood, which was most of the service.

At the apex of the sermon when everyone was caught up in the spoken word and the promises of God, I stood up and walked out of the church. Confused and longing for him I walked back to my car and went home to finish my packing.

I left the house that night, and went to a hotel. The movers had removed most of my personal belongings and the real estate agent would take care of the rest of the items for me and assured me that my vehicle and the other items would be shipped to me in Texas.

That night I slept peacefully and woke up early to take a shuttle to the airport. I couldn't go through with confronting him and saying goodbye. I guess I would have to wait until I am stronger emotionally.

When I arrived at the airport, I checked my bags in at curve side and proceeded to the designated gate.

I decided to stop at one of the coffee stands and get a cup of coffee for my morning "pick me up" so I could stay awake, and work on finding a place to live when I arrived. There were some options but I wanted to explore more.

When I boarded the plane, most of the first class passengers had already been seated. I made my way down the aisle and located my seat. Across the aisle, two men were seated. One of the men was Terrence.

If the floor of the plane would open up I would definitely fall through it right now, I thought. How could I have chosen the exact flight, and where is he going?

I laid back into my seat and closed my eyes as tight as I could to prohibit any light from entering. I positioned my body so that I could not risk even a glance of him and prayed that he would not make any type of gesture to speak to me.

The flight was long and we made one stop before we finally arrived at our destination. It was obvious that we were headed in the same direction because when we arrived at the first stop, he remained in the same seat.

Terrence never attempted to acknowledge or try to talk to me. As conflicted as that felt I was somewhat grateful for that. He was a man that would never impose or attempt to force me into any interaction with him especially in the presence of other preachers. I had that on my side because he was a private man and respected the privacy of others.

When the plane landed and most of the passengers departed the plane, I looked in his direction to see if he was still seated. I could not see his entire body because a woman had made her way from the back of the plane and moved into the seat next to him where the last passenger had been sitting.

I overheard them talking about her reservations and that she was able to get the assigned seat next to him. He stood up and attentively helped her to get situated next to him. He then leaned over, buckled her seat belt, and turned all of his attention to her. It was obvious that she had to be someone that was traveling with him and more than a church member from the interaction between them. I became jealous.

The flight into Texas was a smooth one and I spent the rest of the flight on the internet searching for my new home. I never looked in Terrence's direction throughout the flight.

When the plane landed at our destination, I waited until all of the passengers departed the flight. I made my way to the baggage claim to retrieve my luggage. When I got to the baggage claim, I noticed that he was standing to the other side of the room in deep conversation with the woman. I located my bags and walked outside to take the shuttle to the hotel. I found a seat in the back of the shuttle and laid my head back because suddenly I had gotten a headache, and wanted nothing more but to get to the hotel and lie down.

When I looked up again, Terrence and the woman were seated in the front of the shuttle.

Damn, I said, I hope the hell they are not going to the same hotel. They were.

The line in the hotel check-in was long. It was apparent that there was some type of convention in the city. I prayed to God that it was almost over. Hell is following me, I thought to myself.

Terrence was in line ahead of me and never once did he look back or glance in my direction.

It felt as if I had been discarded like an old shoe. It had been many months since I had spoken to or even interacted with him. I had left the city without any explanation and made no effort to contact him in my absence. I had deserted my relationship with him for reasons not known to him, and now it was his turn to ignore me. I had cause, but would it have changed anything, I thought.

I checked in and went to my room. The room was stuffy and I felt like I could not breathe. I turned on the air and opened the window curtains. The sun was shining so bright and I just wanted to lie in front of the window and soak as much of it as I could.

I took a shower and threw on my favorite torn up jeans across the knees and thighs and an old faded out college tee shirt and shower shoes. I needed a cigarette and went down to the lobby to purchase a pack, and go outside in the fresh air to smoke. I had not had a cigarette for days and crazed to taste the nicotine.

I made my way down the elevator and into the lobby specialty shop and purchased a pack of cigarettes, and headed for the front door of the hotel. The weather was perfect although it was sticky and humid this evening.

I found a place to sit on the curve away from the entrance of the hotel and stretched my legs out to enjoy the relaxation while satisfying my craze for nicotine.

In deep thought, I had not noticed that a crowd of people had come out of the hotel and was entering limousines and other vehicles all dressed up for Sunday service, even though it was not Sunday. In the midst of this crowd, there stood Terrence surrounded by the group. I sat up and decided it was time to escape and leave before I was seen. I was not dressed for the occasion and I must have looked like a homeless person waiting to beg for a quarter for dinner.

I put out my cigarette, got up from the curve and brushed off the dirt that clanged to my pants. I began to make my way around to the parking lot of the hotel and just walk for a while.

Before I could reach the parking lot, I heard someone call out my name. It was Terrence. I stood and froze. He was walking directly towards me. I felt the *panic* start from my head and move slowly down my body. When he reached where I was standing, I turned around to him, and smiled. "Hello," I said, *"What the hell do you want?"*

"Why are you doing this?"
"What?" I asked. "Ignoring your ass, if that is what you are referring to."
"Go back to your groupies you jackass and leave me alone; I don't want no part of your lying ass."

I walked back toward the lobby entrance and never looked back. When I got to the door, some man asked if I was okay and needed help. *"Do I look like I need your help,"* I replied, and continued my way through the lobby and up to my room.

I thought, I should take my deranged self to church and sit right next to his concubines because we had a lot in common. Maybe there were assigned seats for all of us. The front row perhaps, I thought with a smile.

I was so angry — hearing his voice infuriated me. I knew that I was angry because I was hurt. Perhaps, I was insane and was in denial. Why did he still have the ability to control my emotions, and why would I allow him to control them, I questioned myself repeatedly.

I suddenly felt tired and exhausted. I would have loved to attend church tonight and thought it was a good idea. I turned on the television, laid across the bed, and fell asleep with the television drowning out the emptiness of the room.

Later that night, I got hungry and was crazing for some macaroni and cheese and the kitchen had closed. I called down for a taxi to the take me to the nearest grocery store or any place I could get something to eat. I washed my face and threw back on the same clothes I had on earlier that evening. I made my way down to the front lobby and took the taxi to the nearest store. I bought my macaroni and cheese, nachos and a case of soda and a cup of coffee full of sugar.

There was nothing like nachos before bed, and I felt like pigging out to satisfy myself. Since my office hours would not start until Noon the next day I just wanted to kick back and enjoy the evening, alone.

When I got out of the taxi the front of the lobby was not crowded, just a few people standing outside lying about whatever. These days I had developed a sense of perception when it came to identifying liars.

I walked through the lobby thinking about my goodies, and wishing that I had gotten something for the indigestion that I would experience before bedtime.

For some reason, I glanced to my left and observed that there were several men sitting in chairs in deep discussion. When I got closer to the men, there was Terrence pretending to be listening and starring directly at me. His eyes had been following me since I entered the door of the hotel lobby.

I matched his glance, turned and continued to the elevator, which was my escape route to my room. I hated this man and wished he would drop dead right in the lobby. Not literally hate him, *but it would be okay for him to suffer a little*, and if he would die who would I have to hate. I snickered to myself, got on the elevator, and went to my room.

Around 2am, after I had finished my late night meal I decided to take another shower, brush my teeth, and look at my face in the mirror to examine my skin. I needed some moisture in my skin, there were signs of stress and the last thing I wanted was to look how I was feeling.

Before I could finish the examination, there was a knock on the door. I went to the door, stood behind the locked door, and asked, "Who is it? You have the wrong room." "*It's me,*" Terrence said. "Open the door." "*Go back to your madam because I am sure she is waiting for you in the room.*" "Open this door," he said. I stood there for a moment, still angry from earlier and decided it was time he knew that I hated his sorry ass.

I opened the door. "May I help you?" I said. *"Don't try and get funny with me okay,"* his voice was angry. *"What are you doing here in Texas?"* he asked. "None of your business and why should you care?" "Go back to where you came from and leave me alone." I said. There were other choice words I could have used but I was not going to test him tonight.

"We need to talk, what has gotten in to you?" "The devil remember; isn't that what you refer to me as, the devils daughter?"

I walked back to the bed pushed all of the bags and left overs on the floor and got under the covers.

"When you leave close the door behind you and lose my room number."

He sat on the bed and laid his head on my back. "Bernadette, you got to tell me what happened to you, why did you stop communicating with me?"

"Why I stopped communicating with you, do you really want to know?"

"Stand up and let me get out of the bed," I said and *"I can show you better than I can tell you."*

I stood up, turned all of the lights on in the room, and lifted up my tee shirt. He looked at all of the scars on my stomach, bottom side, and just sat on the bed and starred. *"This is what happened,"* I said and started to scream uncontrollable. *"You are what happened to me! I hate you."*

Terrence stood at the side of the bed and starred at me with an indescribable look, and I did not know whether it was shock, pain, or fear.

CHAPTER 12

NO TURNING BACK

At that moment and time, I knew that there was no turning back. We both had been careless in our lust for each other and I had an abnormal pregnancy, and suffered as a result of it. I knew that he was not the one to blame but I had to make him feel as guilty as I was.

I told him about the pregnancy, the complications and my near death experience. We talked about my feelings during those days and the last time that we made love.

"How many months were you pregnant before the surgery?" he asked. Long enough for the doctor to identify our child as a boy," I replied.

He sat down on the bed and put both of his hands up to his head. I wanted to reach out and touch him but my emotions would not allow me. Too much had happened between us and I felt that he had abandoned our relationship before I got pregnant.

"Did you name our son," he asked, "Yes," I replied, he is named after his father.

"How could this have happened Bernadette," he asked. "How could what have happened?" I asked.

"How could we let this happen, how could I not know about this, and how come you refused to let me in on what was going on with your health, your life, and most of all this move to Texas?" He asked.

"Terrence you know as well as I do that you never

"CHURCH GIRLS" the Seduction of Religion

loved me and our association was only a convenience for you," I responded.

"Terrence, now you know all the reasons I left and disappeared. The last time I saw you we were good together. We made love to each other and it was wonderful. I will cherish what we had regardless of it being wrong," I said. "I believe that our son was conceived the last time we made love and he was conceived out of my love for you. I don't hate you and I pray that you don't hate me."

Terrence stood up and walked toward me. I had sat in a nearby chair too weak to continue the conversation and too week to explain any further. He tried to pull me in to his arms but it was too late for that, he was finally out of my life, I thought, and there was no going back. I wanted nothing to do with him. I had relinquished my position to another female who he wanted at his beckoning call and I was done with that, I could do better.

"You have the answer to your question now, so why don't you leave me alone. I hate what we did to each other and I pray you understand." "Pray I understand," he said. "Pray, I understand. Understand what? - that you are a liar and deceitful and that you are evil enough to withhold a pregnancy from me because you are so evil?" He screamed.
"Terrence you do not know love or know what love is all about because you are selfish and self-serving, caught up in yourself and your fame and fortune as a minister," I replied. "I am not the one that is evil, hateful and deceitful, you are. Why do you care about our son or me? I don't blame you for anything and I feel that this was my punishment from God and not yours," I said.
"Terrence, I have forgiven you and myself. I do not want you

thinking that you were the blame for all of my problems even though I was vulnerable at the time of our meeting, and me thinking that you could love me and care for me. I forgive you for using me to handle all of your legal dirt even when I did get paid for it. I forgive you for leaving me at night and going to another woman later that night. I forgive you for lying about your relationships with other women. I forgive you for pretending you were concerned about me all of these years, knowing it was only pretense on your part to get what you needed and wanted without having to work for it.

Frankly, I continued, I don't understand why God would still have his hands on you, but it is not left up to me to judge you. God is going to punish you as he has me. You are not to blame for my actions, only I am to blame and I have no authority over your life to decide what your punishment will be. Mine was the loss of our child and almost my life.

I forgive you for not being there for me because you did not know it, I forgive you for flaunting the women in my face, I forgive you for the times you left my bed and did not say goodbye. I forgive you for letting me go home some nights by myself while you are laid up with someone else that should have been me, I forgive you, and so you got it, just leave and let me live my life in peace.

Terrence, I will always love you and thank you for being there during a part of my life when I lost my will to going on. Even though your being there had a different agenda, you were still there and I will always love you for that.

When you get a chance go visit our baby's gravesite, I am sure he would love to meet his father," I said. I got back into the bed; I was so weak and started crying. I was exhausted and just wanted to sleep. This was one of the most traumatic days of my life; I felt helpless, and alone in the world and at the time he was the only one with whom I could share this secret.

"CHURCH GIRLS" the Seduction of Religion

I went back to the bed and laid down, pulling the covers over my body. I was exhausted and confused. I wanted to curl up and disappear. He reached over to touch me and I just laid there too weak to move. He pulled the covers back, lifted my shirt and laid his head on my stomach. We both laid there in silence for what seemed like an eternity. He got up from the bed and walked toward the door, "Terrence, did you ever love me," I asked. "Good night Bernadette," he said. He never answered my question. I heard the door close behind him as I turned over and went to sleep.

I woke the next morning feeling alive and full of energy. It was one of the most peaceful and restful nights I had experienced in a long time. I did not see him again for six months nor did we communicate.

I started my new career and loved being in Texas. I loved the wide-open country and the people were so different from the people on the East Coast. The folks that surrounded me minded their own affairs and never imposed on each other for anything.

I worked with the immigrants and with charter schools to set up school for immigrants who were English deficient.

During the day I worked, and after I left the office I would work in my garden as my puppy ran around digging in the yard. In the evening, I would lay in the Jacuzzi that I had installed in my back yard and listen to the sounds of the birds chirping. Life was simple and I loved it.

There was not much time to think of my past life or what happened with me. I still loved Terrence and would always want to feel his touch but I knew it would not happen any time in the near future, if at all.

In looking back over our relationship he had not been formerly introduced to my parents or any of my family members, however, I had briefly met his parents.

After a year of not seeing him, I had heard that he decided to take some time off from preaching, why I don't know. I never tried to inquire into his personal life after our relationship even though I would always be concerned about him.

You see, loving him was special to me and leaving him was what I had to do to survive mentally, physical and spiritual. I became obsessed with Terrence and it was not healthy for either of us.

This man controlled me on a very deep level; if he said jump, my reply was how high? If he needed sex, I made myself available. I loved him in any way he wanted. Unconsciously, Terrence was my "black god" and certainly, this wasn't pleasing to GOD to make this man my idol.

I did many things I am not proud of; people were hurt, I acted foolish sometimes and said some things I wish could be taken back, but I cannot undo the past. I can only try to move forward and purpose not to repeat this horrific mistake ever.

In between our relationship, I had been involved with a very special man whom I wanted to love but could not. It was hard for me to pretend to love, and all the time I would have been doing the same thing to him as Terrence had done to me.

"CHURCH GIRLS" the Seduction of Religion

I would be using him and abusing his kindness towards me.

I had no desire to make love to this man because I feared the past. He deserved more than I could give or was willing to give at this point in my life. I felt unworthy to enter into a relationship and knew that I did not have the ability to love again, and did not want the problems that went along with that feeling. After being involved with Terrence, I knew that no man could touch my body and make me feel the way he did.

There would be nobody else. He had become a part of me, a part of my soul and I could not break loose even if I tried.

After a year, Terrence reentered the church circle and began to minister throughout the country and overseas. His ministry began to grow fast and he became a major household name. Whenever I heard he was coming to Texas, I would make it my business to travel to another part of Texas for the week or the weekend. I did not trust myself. I traveled throughout Texas working with immigrants so it was easy just to disappear for a few days or even a week and it did not seem abnormal.

I had gotten used to living in motels because my entire visits out of the city resulted in me staying overnight. Once every month I would fly to California and drive to La Vegas to tour the casinos and shops, and then make my way to Beverly Hills to do my wish list of clothing I wanted to purchase for special occasions and formal functions.

Colleagues whom I worked with invited me out frequently. I joined a small church of 100 members and became active in the church, teaching Sunday school and planning and participating in mission trips to Arizona, and New Mexico.

Life was beginning to show some signs of a new vitality for me and I was waiting in expectation to receive it.

I would take trips to Japan to visit my son, to Florida to visit my parents and once to Alaska to visit an old classmate.

I was free and uninhibited in my life style and loved it. I was careful with not getting involved in any type of relationship, especially one that required time and nurturing. My soul needed to breathe. I was so grateful to God for not allowing me to succumb and die in a deteriorated state; there were moments I didn't think I would live to see another morning.

Some will pass judgment on me, and quite frankly I don't care, but there were a couple of male companions that I always kept on hold just in case I got an urge to satisfy whatever sexual needs that may have developed.

After sometime had passed I became emotionally strong. I was strong enough to attend a revival where Terrence was ministering.

It's amazing that a practicing sinner could still hear from God and bring the house down with a sermon. I didn't get it then and don't understand it now but once again, who am I to lay judgment?

I would sit in the far back of the church and only attend the services if the congregation was huge. I would not let myself attend small church services because I did not want Terrence to know of my presence in the church.

On one occasion, he knew I was in service and sent me an email telling me that it was good to see me in the service, and I looked well. I never responded to the email because one email would lead to another, and I was not ready to face him after our last visit together, which was not a pleasant one.

I was tired of cussing him out, swearing before God and reopening wounds I thought were healing while trying to have a platonic relationship with this man. He wasn't worth that degree of stress in my life.

Even though I did not attend all of his services when he came to Texas, I never missed seeing him on one of the church channels. I could miss him from a distance, which was the safest thing for me to do.

Of course, I wondered how the international television audience would respond if they knew what type of man he really was, that he slept with multiple women, had numerous children outside of wedlock, and a common-law wife (it there is such a thing in the sight God). That he used women to further his ministry, was engaged to five women during the nine years of our relationship, and a host of other craziness.

He knew where I was and if he wanted to get in touch with me he could, but both of us knew it would end up tragic.

Each day brought different adventures in my daily routine. I never regretted having moved from the East Coast and did not miss the *day-to-day* routines.

Our connection was extremely conflicting – my office was still handling certain legal work for his ministry and no matter how I felt personally, I could not allow my firm to lower its standards just because he was a jackass. I continued to provide legal advice to him but only through his office staff, which was the go-between for us. Communication was tense … we tried to keep everything on a professional level. Quick and to the point.

He would forward any information required to complete a project and I would complete and forward back to his office for review. We remained cordial to each other and he never mentioned what I had told him in the hotel that night (about the baby). It was as if none of it had ever happened and both wanted to move forward with our lives.

Not seeing him did not last for long because he had his office to schedule a meeting with me on his next visit to Texas, which would be in a month.

I had to prepare what he needed to close on some property he was looking to purchase and we had to meet *face-to-face* to finalize the documents, have them notarized and filed while he was in Texas.

I convinced myself there would not be a problem with meeting him because it had been over a year since we were alone in a hotel room, and I was fine with agreeing to meet him.

When he landed in Texas, I met him at the airport and we had lunch and finalized all of the documents that were needed to purchase the property he was buying. It was a pleasant visit and he looked well even though he had lost a lot of weight.

"How are you Bernadette," he asked. "I am doing great," I replied.

As we were going over the papers, he pulled his chair next to mine and placed his arm around the back of my chair. I felt a little uncomfortable sitting so close to him but knew that I had to endure it. We were not strangers to our feelings and the emotional vibrations between us.

Terrence has always entrusted his legal matters to me and rarely questioned my advice. We both were okay with our professional relationship without the personal strings attached. I wanted to ask him about his life and his relations but was fearful of the answer. Part of me wanted to become a part of his life again, while the other part was in total disagreement.

"Where are you going after you leave me?" He asked. "I will never leave you I said and reached in with my shoulder to nudge his."

"Great," he said, and we both smiled.

Terrence never really asked questions he did not know the answer to or felt he did not know the answer to. He knew that I couldn't stay in a relationship with him based on the lies of our relationship and his unfaithfulness.

I have always wondered if I made more out of the relationship that I shouldn't have. Did I prompt him to get personally involved with me, or did I appear to be such a needy and weak female that he felt this was the ideal situation where he would benefit the most? I am not sure.

In looking back over our relationship, I would have never gotten involved with him if I had remained a married woman, even if he had retained me as his attorney.

This relationship crystalized several things —I had in fact lost my way and though I had always respected the church and its leaders, and would have never been emotionally involved with a preacher, this experience cancelled out everything that was once sacred.

Terrence was the exception— a rule breaker.

After we finalized all of the documents, Terrence stood up and asked to walk me to my car. I accepted the gesture and it felt good for us to talk without all the baggage that a relationship brings to the table.

When we walked outside of the airport and into the parking lot, we stood there for an hour and talked. He felt it necessary to catch me up on the latest church news. There was apparently no change.

He leaned against the car with his arms folded, and I stood in front of him talking a mile a minute about my work and the children that I work with in the English deficiency classes.

All the time that I was talking, he never interrupted me but appeared to be attentive to all of my stories and history lessons about the immigrant population that I represented. Occasionally he would laugh at some of my animations and ask me to elaborate more about certain topics.

"I have been talking on and on," I said. "Where is your ride?" I asked.

"I rented a car and will be driving myself to my hotel. I did not want to be picked up because I did not know how long this meeting with you would take," he replied.

I offered to drive him to the rental car section at the airport, and he accepted. He reached over for the keys as he usually did when we were together, and I handed them over gracefully.

When we got in the car, he turned on the radio and located a radio station that played music we both enjoyed. The visit felt right and we were attempting to work through a long history of pain.

I asked about certain biblical scriptures and he explained them to me. He asked if I attended a church and I told him about a small church I was attending. He asked questions about the preacher and the congregation and I told him that the minister was over the age of 80, and that I was the youngest member of the congregation.

I knew that this information would please him and the questions about the church was his way of finding out my church affiliation.

"Terrence you don't have to worry about me cheating on you with another preacher," I said. As I threw up both my arms, I bellowed out, "I have been redeemed."

When we arrived at the rental car place, I waited until he had checked in and got the keys to the assigned car. I watched him as he took his luggage from my car and carried it over to the rental car. I wanted to go with him, to be near him for the balance of the day, night and each day and night after that. I knew it was not possible and the harm would be even greater than before.

I got out of the car and went around to the driver side to get in. I stood there for a few minutes until he had all of his bags placed in the trunk.

Terrence walked back to the car and stood in front of me. "You know that I love you and miss you," he said. "*I also want you to know that I realize that sometimes you need me and there is no harm in admitting it or picking up the phone and calling me or emailing me to let me know that you are okay,*" he said.

I nodded my head. Terrence reached over and kissed me on the forehead and we both got in our vehicles and drove away.

CHAPTER 13

THE
TELEPHONE CALL

During the time that I was traveling around the country after my surgery, I was in contact with old law school alumni in Texas who had agreed to handle all of Terrence's legal affairs for the exception of certain property deals. I felt that I owed this to Terrence to make every effort to keep his legal affairs private and place them in the hands of someone that I trusted. Later on in the relationship between Terrence and the attorney, Terrence agreed to retain him for all legal services.

I was pleased with the direction that both of our lives were headed. Terrence seemed to be settling down and focusing more on building his ministry on his own strengths as a bishop. I had always hoped and prayed that he would finally realize that he was truly a chosen man of God, and with that came great responsibility.

Yes, I missed him but it was a warm and fuzzy type of missing him. For years I had stop getting the orgasms when I thought of him but the flutters still remained in my stomach when I spoke to him.

Three days each week, my assignment was to go the fields and interview immigrants. Each week my caseload appeared to increase. This particular Monday morning I began to sense that something was wrong and I couldn't shake the feeling.

I was sitting at my desk, which was an old fold up table that I transported in my car whenever I interviewed immigrants at the edge of the fields where they worked, when my cell phone rang.

When I answered the telephone, I was surprised to

"CHURCH GIRLS" the Seduction of Religion

hear the voice of the Texas attorney who was handling all of Terrence's legal matters.

"*Hello there*" I said, "*what's up?*"

"*It seems like it is you because you are out traveling around Texas while I am here slaving.*"

"*Poor baby,*" I said jokingly.

"*How are things going these days with the office, and your clients and the girls and the new car I heard you had just purchased?*"

"*When are you going to get married anyways?*" I said.

"*Just as soon as you decide you are tired of running away from me and resolve to settle down and let's raise a family.*"

We both laughed because he was an old nut and should have retired twenty years ago.

"Listen," he said, "*I just got a call from your friend the preacher. You know I have been working with you on his cases for months and things have been going good. I have put in a lot of travel closing property deals for him and he has been more than a stellar client. Despite his craziness in his personal life, the man is quite a business man and knows how to handle himself.*"

"Get to the point, I said, what has he done this time?"

"Well," he started, "*it seems that he decided to get involve with the wife of one of his minister associates, which had been going on for some time. He made promises to the female, they traveled together; she met him in different cities and also traveled with him overseas and spent a week at some hot vacation spot over in Hawaii.*"

"So?"

"The first lady as you call them decided she had enough of her boring life and told her husband that she was leaving, and told him all about the relationship with your boy. You are not going to believe this, the first lady got pregnant and now in a few months he will be the proud father of a baby girl. Of course he said that it is not his baby but is not denying the affair."

Wow, Terrence really made a mess out this one…

"This is not the worse, he also was involved with another young female at the church and she delivered a baby girl some fifteen months ago. He is a family man with child, he said."

I held the phone so tight that it could have crumbled in my hand. "Okay, why are you calling me?" I said. "He wanted me to talk to you and see what you thought he should do. This will ruin his ministry and if all of it is true, it will ruin many lives. He has finally sealed his faith in ministry, I think," he said.

"Let me think about this and get back to you, after all he did not rape anyone. He sexed another stupid female who thought she was in love and following the anointing, chasing fame and probably has been a groupie for ministers on the circuit, and intentionally got pregnant," I said.

"Yea," he said, "you have always said that the anointing draws people, and this time it has drawn all the way to his wallet for the next 18 years times two"…

I hung up the telephone and completed my interviews; I put it in the back of my mind for the rest of the day. I refused to allow any disturbance to enter my spirit; perhaps last year

"CHURCH GIRLS" the Seduction of Religion

I'd have fallen out, wasted time being angry, but not today.

I was not going to have my joy disturbed and especially by this uncommitted preacher. Whatever I gave him in the past was all I planned to invest with him going forward. He just happened to be one of those preachers who could not keep his pants on or, strong enough to resist any urges to have sex with any willing participant.

The drive back to my motel was a short one, and I enjoyed the smell of the air during planting season and the sound of the machinery in the fields. It reminded me of home, which I missed so much in the south during this time of the year.

The motel where I stayed was referred to as a fleabag motel. This is where some of my clients stayed during the seasonal work. Some evenings I would sit outside the motel room and watch them as they cooked on the grill and the children running around playing, and chasing the night as I use to do when I was a child.

They would offer me food, and I never refused because it seemed rude not to accept. Although I did not eat it, I would put it in a cooler that I carried with me and give it to one of the children the next day, or that same night if there was someone who appeared to be hungry from another family.

"Goodnight," I said, to all of the people who were outside and who had provided me entertainment for the evening. I loved being here me thought and emptied my coffee cup and went back into my room.

After I took my bath, I decided to telephone Terrence. I had already known what I would say to him because it had been said many times before.

The phone rings two times before he picked it up. *"Hello gorgeous,"* he said. *"How are you doing?"* I said. *"I am doing okay just a little tired these days."* I'm not big on small talk but wanting to be civil engaged in the banter.

"Have you been taking your vitamins?" I asked trying to be civil. *"You know I have but I just cannot shake being this tired."* *"May be from all the traveling because it seems like I am doing nothing but traveling."*

"You need to take leave and rest for a few months. The natives can wait," I said.

"I will take that under advisement," he said and we both laughed.
"By the way, I received a call from my old law partner who has been handling your business; I hear your body parts have gotten themselves tied up lately in a certain first lady."

We talked about his relationship with the minister's wife, and how it all began and when he tried to end it things got impossible because she told him that she was pregnant. He said it was not his baby because he had always been careful. For some reason I believed him. He was not a stupid man just horny and sex crazed. But as the old adage go, every person has a day and it seem like this day fate was paying him back for living a double life. And out of all the people, his friend's wife.

"I believe you," I said. *"This time I really believe you."*

"*I will be in your area in a few days, will you come to church? I would love to see you and maybe we can have dinner out in the open fields. I heard you like open fields these days.*"

I smiled, because we both were thinking the same thing. There were never any conversations without sexual connotations involved.

"*I will see you in church soon. Hey Terrence, you know what my last statement has been to you all of these years about the women the first day I met you, and the first case I ever represented you in?*"
"*Yea,*" he said.
"*A dog does not shit where he has to lay his head.*"
"*Right, see you soon*"; and we both hung up.

I felt good about the conversation because this was the first civil conversation we had in a very long time.

His ministry was in trouble and he could be destroyed because the first lady was married to a man who had a very powerful ministry. Why did this happen? The dishonorable way he disposed of me and now has to ask for help, isn't that something I said to myself.

I turned on the air conditioner that ran very loud to drown out any thoughts of him and tried to fall asleep, but my mind wanted to work.

Not sure why I would even consider helping him nor was it clear if it was the bad boy mad love thing or what - secretly wanting to be attached to someone, I know I could not have.

Anyway, a few seconds later I jumped out of the bed and

called the preacher back.

On one ring, he answered the telephone. *"Hi, it's me again. I just need to be clear as to who the minister really is because I think that I represented someone in a child support case against him."*

We talked and he gave me the minister's name and the name of the church. *"I knew it,"* I screamed, this is the same fool that I settled a case with and afterward he propositioned me and I told him his bank account was not fat enough.

"Well, well, well," I said aloud, *"this guy is finally getting a taste of some of his own medicine."*

"I will set up an appointment with him but I need to travel back to Washington to do it unless he will be traveling somewhere closer, and I can meet him there to discuss a few options you both may have." He thanked me and we hung up.

I traveled in the church circle and had been introduced to many ministers and their wives; I was not a stranger to the church community.

I could not resist being a smart butt… *"The 1st lady get a 'Holla out' from me,"* I said.

CHAPTER 14

I WILL BE YOUR ANGEL

I made all of the arrangements to meet Terrence and the other minister in New Orleans. This would be perfect for me since I wanted to see my parents, because it had been too long from the time when we were together as a family.

I knew there would be no danger of meeting up with him because it was a business trip, and after the meeting, I would head to Florida.

Terrence had purchased an investment property in New Orleans and some years later, moved one of his women into his house, whom he claimed was a house sitter, but I knew better. Many women had been eager to play the part of pretending to be his wife. They would settle for this status and be happy. Me, I wanted no part of that part of his life because he would never be faithful to one woman. He had too many demons and too many hang-ups about marriage and relationships. He knew what type of woman he could count on to manage his affairs and who would be a good little girl, follow directions, and sit home and wait for him to come so they could play house.

Terrence never used money to try to buy any females' attention, definitely not mine. His physical features, mannerism, charm and compassion were his strengths.

He knew how to draw women and men into his circle and dispose of them with grace and charm; not that he was always this tactful, but he certainly knew how. Men would follow him because they thought some of the anointing would transfer to them, and they could meet some other ministers in the church circle to grow their status and ministry, while on the other hand, the women just wanted attention, sex and to be connected and seen in his presence.

"CHURCH GIRLS" the Seduction of Religion

Women *loved* him and men *admired* him. He was a man of distinction and grace but yet deadly to me. I worshiped him and put him before God as I suppose so many other women did and still do.

I had arranged with the minister (*who probably wanted Terrence dead for touching his wife*) to meet in Terrence's room and afterward we would professionally move forward. It wasn't this cut and dry; the meeting was extremely contentious-they cussed at each other and wanted to fight; there was no doubt in mind that if the other minister could get away with killing Terrence for getting his wife pregnant, he would have been dead. Without question.

When I received the telephone call that he was in his room and the other minister was present I felt safe, and I knew I had my emotions under control. It had been over nine months since I had seen Terrence, and I was anxious to see him.

I knocked and he opened the door. He appeared to have lost more weight than the last time I saw him, and appeared thin but not frail.

He greeted me with a kiss on the cheeks and it felt good. "No touching," I said, and we both smiled.

I started the meeting off because I had heard both sides prior to the meeting. Reverend Canon wanted to damage Terrence's reputation, and to prevent him from preaching at any of the churches under his jurisdiction or any of the Baptist churches he was affiliated within the *Baptist convention*.

Reverend Canon was very angry and hostile; he kept interrupting me as I spoke. Before I knew what I was saying, I yelled, "*Shut the hell up both of you because if you do not, I am going to tell both of you to go straight to hell where you both belong right now.*"

The minister said, "*I will not sit here and let you talk to me like that.*" "*Don't,*" I said "*but you will listen when I put your business out in the street about the baby mama case I represented, and you approaching me asking for sex, that is after you rubbed my ass.*"

He sat down and became cordial at that moment . . . they both had too much to lose behind this nonsense and despite having their egos bruised, finding an amicable working arrangement was the *only* answer.

We talked about the problem that they both were facing, I gave my suggestions, and they both agreed. The minister would stay with his wife until the alleged pregnancy was over and act like a very happy father to be, while Terrence would continue preaching in all of the affiliated churches if he was invited. No one would continue entertaining the gossip or try to discredit the other person, and they would not discuss this even with the minister's wife. If the wife wanted to leave and get a divorce, let her and I will handle the divorce.

Terrence agreed to take leave and get some rest until all of the church gossip quieted down. He needed much rest and it showed in his face.

I suggested that he take a trip to some island and enjoy himself, and if he just had to, take one of his concubines with him because I was sure she needed the attention (I said with great pride).

"CHURCH GIRLS" the Seduction of Religion

When we agreed to all of the final details, we went down to the restaurant and had a meal . . . they were both extremely uncomfortable but, Terrence knew he was wrong. After all, he knew the minister and had fellowship with him on several occasions, and why he couldn't keep his pants zipped and not touch another man's wife is beyond me.

Later on, after the minister's divorce was finalized he remarried—the minister married one of Terrence's old concubines. Out of all the women in the world from which they could choose these preachers swapped partners like turning water on from a faucet. It is as if there weren't any other women available except those they have all slept with. The church world had gone crazy and the ministers and congregation with it.

Terrence escorted me to the lobby. We went over his instructions again before I left. My car was parked in the hotel parking lot, which was right outside the hotel lobby.

After the meeting, I said my goodbyes and left to visit my parents. As I was walking to my car, Terrence was standing outside the lobby door watching me until I made it to the car.

"*I thought you were going to stick around and have some drinks with me,*" Terrence said, without looking back I said, "*you know I do not drink and if I did who would do the drinking first, you or me?*"

"*We both could at the same time,*" he said. "*You naughty boy that sure sounds tempting*" I said, and continued toward my car for the long trip to Florida. That man never stop trying to get me back into his bed, I thought.

"*You fresh girl,*" he said.

"*You never complained before*" I said, and threw up my hand and waved good-bye. He yelled, "*I miss you already.* " This time I believed that he did miss me.

It always amazed me how issues between ministers can be resolved so easily especially when they all was possessed with the same demon.

Terrence had grown up under Reverend Canon's ministry; the reverend had taken him under his wings when he was just starting out. The reverend had allowed Terrence to teach/speak at church conventions and revivals when most of the church world had never heard of him, so quite naturally, Terrence having an affair with his wife was the ultimate betrayal.

Now that Terrence is famous, they both had forgotten that they knew of each other indiscretions and now the *"pot wanted to call the kettle black"* as the old folks use to say.

Before I could get on the interstate headed to Florida, Terrence had sent me a text message. All it said was "Thanks!"

"You are absolute welcome"; I said aloud and continued to drive.

The church world is like any other business. Even though it should not be, there is so much competition and cutthroat and jealously. You have ministers who think of themselves as more anointed than others, because I have represented a few of them. I just never understood why the jealously existed because it was God who did the anointing, choosing, calling into ministry and appointing his chosen ones for the type of work he predestined for their lives.

Who am I, I thought to myself, I am just another congregation member who want to be blessed.

I turned onto Interstate 10 in anticipation of seeing my parents. This was a good trip and I hope that the ministers stop their fornicating and adultery, I thought. Then I shook my head; No way, not until Jesus come.

CHAPTER 15

NO MORE DEMONS

I was always amazed how hot the sun was in Florida and how it beamed down directly on my face even while driving in the car.

It felt good to be back at home and on the farm. I had been there a couple of days and long enough to attend Sunday service with my mother but I opted not to participate. The last time I was here, I attended service and was the center of the gossip. Most of the town gossips knew about my bad marriage and some of the horrific things I experienced, but never offered any support. Over 90% of my critics saw how bad I looked the last time I visited but this time I was different. God helped me to get my stride back, it felt so darn good…, and yes, I flaunted it like wearing a beautiful gown to a ball.

Many were jealous because I was so fabulously dressed and driving my new Mercedes Benz and getting all of the stares from the country guys. Who wouldn't be jealous of that? Not merely jealous of the vehicle or the clothes, but just the fact that when I was there the last time I had just come out of a bad marriage and looked just as bad, and most of them wrote me off as dead.

I sat out in the old rocking chair under the oak tree where it must have set for the past twenty years. The tree had to be over a hundred years old and if it could speak, I am sure that it would tell of all of the old stories of adventures of the past years, and the many visitors it had shielded from the sun and rain and the many picnics it had been a part of.

With my eyes closed, I could hear the horses running around in the pasture across the one lane now paved highway (it used to be a dirt street). The chickens that had escaped from the coup were busy pecking corn in the back yard, and probably praying that I would let them have their freedom a little longer before I chased them around and put them back in. I could hear in the distance the sound of tractors and the train that often passed in the back of my parents' house this time of day.

It felt good lying around being lazy and away from the *day-to-day* stressful activities, which I had so enjoyed when I became an attorney many years ago.

I was excited especially about today because my son and his wife were coming to visit and they were traveling with my nephew and his wife, and their 3-month-old son. He was back in the states for a couple of weeks and decided to stop in to visit the grandparents.

When is mama coming back from church, I thought. They could not be having that good of time or have that much church business because there were only a handful of members, and most of them slept through the service.

Before I could finish my thoughts, I heard the old church van pull up in front of the house. I walked over, helped mama down from the van, and waived to the deacon and the old church mothers that were still waiting to be dropped at home by the deacon.

He had to drive slow and stay way under the speed limit of 45 or else they probably would be banging his head with the purses and speaking in tongue. We walked in the house, *arm-in-arm*.

"How was church mama?" I asked. "That boy really delivered a message today and it almost excited me." "Right," I said, "I am sure he did." "How is the wife and children?" I asked. "Fine" she said and "they asked about you." I am sure they did, I thought.

My mother's pastor happened to be my first childhood boyfriend. He was fine back in those days and his eyes could read a woman like a book. I am glad that it was a childhood romance because if it was more than that I could have ended up with seven children, and weighing three hundred pounds like his wife and dragging children behind me holding onto every appendage of my body.

Although he was also over 350 pounds, he was still the ladies' man that he was in the past. If I entertained the thought of flirting with him or attempted to sneak around with him, I am sure that I would have choked, died and gone to heaven for sure because God takes care of babies and fools, and certainly, I am not a baby. The thought gave me chills. God must have a special formula for choosing pastors; that one I would never have guessed.

About four o'clock mama had warmed up the food she had prepared before she went to church. I dared not to touch it because she had her special way of warming food up and I was glad because I did not want to risk destroying her Sunday dinner, because it was a special dinner, and this was the first time mama would be laying eyes on her new grandson.

My great nephew was just as cute as he could be. He had a head full of curly hair and looked just like his father. "Hi mama," my son said as he walked in the door and his wife was coming in behind him holding my great nephew. My nephew and his wife were still out in the car gathering the baby things.

My daughter-in law carefully laid the baby in my arms and he was still fast asleep, and they walked in the kitchen to see mama. I looked down and brushed the baby's hair and moisture from around the nose and forehead.

By this time, the baby reached up and squirmed. This was a sign to locate my niece and give the baby back, but he calmed down and fell back to sleep.

"You are going to be a minister just like your papa aren't you?" I said. "Hi minister." By that time my nephew walked in the door, "just prophesying," I said, and we all laughed.

After dinner, I decided to drive down the country back roads and enjoy the night by listening to the owls and birds, and watch the animals as they jumped across the highway and ran under bushes when they saw the headlights.

I went into the little town to get some ice cream from the gas station. This was my way of relaxing especially since my son and nephew and families had already headed to Georgia to visit their other cousins of the same age. The family is a close family and each generation seemingly got alone.

When I got home, my parents were sitting on the front porch in their own assigned rocking chairs, which they had assigned to themselves many years ago.

"Your phone has been ringing off the hook since you went out,"

mama said. "That is probably my man," I responded. She reached her hand out and tried to pat me on my bottom side but I was too quick for her.

I went in the house and grabbed my phone to check my messages. I had to be back in Texas in two days, there were some emergency hearings and several of my clients were listed for deportation back to Mexico.

I then checked my text messages, no message from the preacher. I guess he was okay.

CHAPTER 16

MAKING A CHOICE

The seasons had gone by fast and we were entering the spring. I had been very busy and had not had time to enough to socialize with anyone, especially the preacher.

Terrence was scheduled to be in Houston this weekend and it was the weekend of my birthday. I was glad he would be in Texas ministering for three days, because two of those days I would not be able to attend since I had to interview in a different area of Texas, which was within miles of Houston.

I sent a text message back to him and told him that I would attend church when I got back and we both agreed to celebrate my birthday together.

We had become cordial these days and both came to the realization that we did not have to be lovers or friends, we just knew that we would be there for each other if there was ever a time to do so. That was more important to me than attempting to define our relationship.

We agreed not to discuss the past or my surgery or the women in his life. The birthday dinner would be about celebration, it was the birth of a new life for me, and reconciliation for him.

The sanctuary was packed as usual when he ministered. I found a seat in the balcony of the church and still was able to get a clear view of him and enjoy the service.

I participated in the service and for once in my life following our differences, I enjoyed actually being back in church and listening to him minister.

I had never heard such an orator and he knew the bible. He knew how to calm the congregation and how to get them excited about Jesus.

After service, I sat around in the sanctuary until he changed his clothes. He was dressed in a pair of black pants and a black tee shirt. Damn, this man look good, I thought. I watched his every move as he walked toward me. He was talking to one of his musicians as they headed down the row I had chosen to sit in after service.

I greeted the musician and then reached over and hugged and kissed the musician and then Terrence.

The musician was going to join us for dinner and I liked the idea, because the musician was always on my side whenever the preacher and I had a disagreement. The musician always thought we had a love hate relationship, to him it was crazy, and we both needed to be institutionalized.

We all packed into my vehicle and headed to a restaurant that was still open. He drove my car because he has never trusted my driving. He put his hand in the middle of my back and opened the passenger door after he had held out his hands for the keys, as usual, I handed the keys over without hesitation.

The ride to the restaurant was a quiet one and he sang as we drove. It appeared that all of us were lost in thought and it felt good to be together again.

The musician broke the silence by asking me about my work. I started talking and couldn't stop talking; on occasions

Terrence would glance over at me, especially when I talked I had to touch and it appeared that I had been touching him and laughing throughout the trip.

When we arrived at the restaurant there was a birthday cake waiting and drinks (non-alcoholic), tropical drinks which I enjoyed.

We ordered my vegetarian dish and they both ordered the Texas steak dinner. The evening was so enjoyable and I began to long for this life again without the drama. I found myself caught up in the moment and it felt good. When I blew out the candles after the restaurant staff sang happy birthday, he reached over and kissed me on the lips. I accepted the kiss and turned my focus to cutting the cake.

I felt a little uncomfortable with the kiss but it was my birthday and I had to be reading something into it. We had not made love for almost two years, and definitely, the sparks had gone out of the relationship for both of us, perhaps one of us, and it was not me.

We drove back to his hotel and my intentions were to ride back to the motel where I was staying. El Paso was quite a distance from Houston and would take me over a day to get back. I did not have to go into the office for two days, which gave me ample time to drive back home.

When we arrived back to Terrence's hotel, we all got out of the car in front of the lobby. I said goodnight to the musician. Terrence came around to the passenger side and put the keys in my hand.

When I reached over to hug him and thank him, he grabbed me by my hand. "*I want you to stay with me tonight,*" he said. I wanted to and he knew it. I just did not think it was a good idea. He then leaned against the car as he has always done; his arms crossed and began to stare at me. That same stare always seemed to convince me of anything. "I just cannot," I said; "we agreed to move forward with our lives and to respect each other's decision."

"I just need you to stay with me tonight," he said emphatically. I did not know what was going on in his life, if anything, but I sensed that there was some type of turmoil and I was about to fall into the pit of hell that I had already dug myself out of.

I waited for him to park the car and we walked back to his room. It was not uncomfortable on the elevator because on the ride up to the floor we held each other and did not speak.

It was apparent that we both needed each other tonight and did not realize that this night would change both of our lives.

When we entered the room, he went through the same rituals that he had always done in the past. I saw no changes in him with me. I would not allow myself to think of him with anyone else. Tonight was just between our demons and us.

He turned on a news station, took off his clothes and went in the bathroom to turn on the tub for our routine bath with each other. He yelled back, "do you still shave like I taught you?" "You did not teach me anything and, the answer is yes."

We both laughed; *"Country girl,"* he said, *"I taught you everything that you know. You know you were country backward until I met you."*

"Right," I said.

I took off my shoes, grabbed the remote, and started flipping channels. He came out, pulled me off the bed, and led me into the bathroom.

"Take off your clothes and let me examine your shaving techniques."

Unable to resist, I took off my clothes and when I looked down at him, his eyes were focused on the scars on my stomach.

Trying to take his focus off me, I reached out for him to take my hand and lure me down in the water.

"Are you okay, really okay with this?" he asked. "Yes" I said. I laid my hand on his leg and leaned back against him. What happened to my resolution to move on is beyond me . . . I was still possessed by him and wanted him to make me feel good, feel loved and needed.

I felt so weak, knowing in my heart this wasn't the right decision, but found myself just wanting to be loved even if it was for the last time. I know something was missing in my soul but I was willing to submit to him and do whatever he needed. I wanted him to make me feel good and he was the only man that could do that. He was the only man I wanted.

I have heard that time heals all things; however it was

not true for me. Being with Terrence now and then had been the only time that I needed or wanted.

I was not inhibited with him as I had been with my husband and the other men in my life. I was not a risk taker with my health so I was selective in my sex partners, and I could count on one hand the number of men I have ever slept with.

We dried off and went to the sofa to sit down. I grabbed my top and put it on and sat on the sofa, crossed my legs on the cushion while he pulled and grabbed his phone and listened to his messages. He made a telephone call to his office (yeah right), and spoke with his secretary for a couple of minutes and in his sexy voice said good night. I thought this better be a goodnight because this fool is still full of shit.

In the months before the surgery, when things were hot and heavy with us, as a birthday present to him I had decided to get a tattoo on my stomach of a rose. The rose extended from the top of my navel with the stem painted down to the top of my female organ, and the last initial of his name on one of my shoulders. I was wild about this man and I was branded.

He laid the phone down and reached over to turn the light off and turn on the radio. It never failed he always turned on music. I think it probably relaxed him it certainly did me.

"Are you sure you are okay with this?" I said "yes," and it was the best sex I had ever had in my life, my body was on fire. He felt every inch of my body and flipped me like pancakes. After we made love and both were exhausted, I laid on top of him, reached up, and locked my fingers in both of his hands, which were stretched out. I began to feel a fear come over me and felt such anxiety that I wanted to run.

"What's the matter?" he asked. "Nothing." I said. He reached up, kissed me, laid me on my back, and entered my body. The deep penetration caused both of us to climax at the same time. The feeling would not pass even while we were making love.

He must have felt the same way because all of a sudden he stopped talking and rolled over on his back, and started looking up at the ceiling. He reached over to me and patted my leg, kissed me on the lips and got off the bed and went into the bathroom.

When he returned he went to the desk where he had placed his laptop, opened it and started to check his messages. Occasionally he would look over at me and then back to the laptop. I wanted to get up and put my clothes on and run out of there but something or someone was holding me there and it was not him.

I climbed off the bed, went over, put both of my arms around his neck, and kissed his neck, and then I lifted his left arm and put my head on his lap. He was sitting there calm and seemed to be okay. He lowered his head and kissed me on the top of the head. "*I Love you*," he said. That was the first time I had ever heard him say that he loved me and I believed it to be true. Our relationship was never about love.

"I have to go," I said. "I want to get back." I got dressed and as he sat back and watched me, not my body but my face.

He walked me to the car even though it was daylight because we had been hours of making love and time was not important to either of us.

While I was driving back, I got a very funny feeling in my stomach. I have heard church people say that your spirit lies within your stomach walls and you know when something is about to happen, because you feel it in your stomach.

Feeling immensely disturbed in my spirit I pulled in the next service station and parked. I had to call or text him and repeat what I was hearing in my head and I am sure he heard the same thing.

"Baby," I said, "*I just had to call you because it seemed to be necessary right now to talk to you about these feelings. I am frightened and have been since we made love. Something is telling me to tell you that God is not pleased with us and is frowning upon our fornication and if we touch each other again we will truly die, not only a spiritual death but also physical death. I cannot do this anymore, I am afraid and I know this is true. Also we are going to be punished.*"

The phone was silent for a few minutes and he said, "*I will call you later and we can talk.*"

When I got home, I went straight to my bed, got under the covers, and slept. I was exhausted.

CHAPTER 17

IT IS FINALLY OVER AGAINST OUR CHOICE

That evening we talked and he told me that he had experienced the same feelings that I had. I did not want to believe that I could not touch him again without harder consequences that I had experienced in the past. I was not going to regret last night, I loved him, and that was that. I knew that I was not the only female in his life but did not care, and I was willing to take whatever time he could give me and be content with it. His attention would only be a supplement to my time and that was okay.

"Are you coming to church tonight?" he asked. The same way as he as always done.

"Yes, I think I can make it but I am so tired."

"Tonight, I think I will stay in the hotel; I will book my reservations and drive over to church afterward.

I packed my overnight bag, grabbed a suit and sandals with heels, and headed for the door. It was getting dark outside but I still had time to make it to the hotel, shower and change and make it to the church before he could finish reading his scriptures.

I hated to sit through all of that church business and the singing excited me too much.

When I arrived at the church, I found a seat in the back of the church as usual. I did not feel like going to the balcony and I stayed downstairs.

He was addressing the congregation when I entered the church and sat down. He paused and said, *"I see you and I'm glad you could make it.*" He then said, "*A friend of mine just walked in and I want to acknowledge he*r." He asked me to stand up and he introduced me as his attorney. This had been a frequent acknowledgment in the past and for some reason he thought that it should continue whenever I came to church to hear him minister.

Following service, I drove back to the hotel. I just wanted to see him and hear what he had to say about what I told him earlier.

I sat on the bed and began to weep and feel sorry for myself. I would not let myself ask questions, like what is wrong with you, or say you are a fool, why did you let him back in your spirit, and you are insane aren't you?

I decided to get up from the bed and pull myself together so he would not see me in such a foolish state of mind. I was a grown woman and experienced in life. I removed my makeup and put some eye drops in my eyes. This was not out of character for me to cry because it had been happening since the day we met.

So I showered and got dressed, not in my pajamas, but in my shorts and a top. I sat down to regroup and stretched out on the bed again until I heard the key in the door. I had left him a key at the front desk and was expecting him after he socialized with the other ministers and talked business.

"Hi," he said, "are you asleep yet?" "No, because I wanted to be awake when you got here," I said. I looked over at the clock, "you got finished early," I said. He did not respond but said after he scanned my body, "come talk to me while I take a shower." I went into the bathroom with him and sat on the commode while he showered.

"Terrence what are we going to do?" I asked.

"Do about what?" he said.

"What I said to you this morning about the feelings after we made love."

"We have to not make love again," he said. *"You keep your pants on tonight and I will sleep in my own room."*

"I am serious."
"So am I," he said. *"Let's go get some breakfast."* I slipped on some shower shoes and headed for the door.

"Where are you going looking like that?" "To breakfast" I said. *"You are too country,"* he said and we left for breakfast.

During breakfast we talked about both of our concerns and he told me that several nights before that at another church, a minister prophesied by God regarding a relationship.

He said, the minister said 'there was a female that God had forbid in his life and the female was chosen by God.'

"Did he tell you the name of the female," I asked. *"No,"* he said *"but later he did confirm it was you." "What do you mean, confirm?"* I said.

"CHURCH GIRLS" the Seduction of Religion

"It's you," he said, and "I have known this for a long time. I just needed to make love to you again and I was willing to sacrifice it because God has always forgiven me in the past for my transgressions with everyone except you."

I reached out to touch his hand but he moved it away slowly. We drove back to the hotel, parked the car, and walked to the lobby and up to his room.

He opened the door and we walked in in silence. He went into the bathroom, began to gather all of his personal items, and then started to pack; he had his suitcase on the bed and began to assemble all of his clothes and shoes. I laid on the bed, pulled the cover over my body, and drifted off to sleep. He entered the room, and I heard him say, "*And then she sleeps.*" "What did you say?" I asked. "*Nothing*" he said, "*I was just thinking out loud.*"

I sat up on the bed, stretched out my arms, and stretched. "*I think I will go back to my room and get ready to go also.*" "No," he said, "*just stay here until I pack. You were serious when you said that you had to leave me.*"

"No not leave you, but to leave. I have a six o'clock flight and have to be in church in Chicago tonight."

"When are you coming back to Texas?" I asked, "I don't know," and he walked over and kissed me on my forehead but before he could move away from me I reached for him and he pulled me in and kissed me on the lips.

"*I am going to walk you to the elevator now,*" he said. "*We can talk later; I have to finish packing because the deacon will be here soon to give me a ride to the airport.*"

We walked to the elevator in silence. When we reached the elevator, he reached down and touched my fingers with such a gentle touch. *"Let's ask God what we should do. Maybe it is time to get married."*

But this was not to be.

Stay tuned for future updates - where they are now… follow on Twitter @churchgirls15. You won't believe the outcome.

APPENDIX A

A Church Girl Demonized

Take little Anna Mae Bullock (Tina Turner) as an example of a marvelous creation of God who was badly hurt by a small rural local church when she was merely a girl. Little Anna Mae was the only little girl in the church choir, consisting of older teens and adults in a Negro church, if this beautiful term may be so employed, to the credit of "blacks."

Now the only music she understood in the home was bar singing—rhythm and blues and jazz. Yet her church had not embraced such cultural forms of music, but clung to pure, traditional church music.

Reared in the broken home of "party girls" with the exception of her grandmother who was truly a righteous woman of God, it is possible that little Anna Mae was taken advantage of in the most damaging manner. There is much that is unknown or revealed about her childhood.

However, many girls in little Anna Mae's predicament are indeed hurt in such manners. Many of them search for sanctuary in the community of "faith" at local churches. They are open to finding who God is. Some find Him. Yet for many, while in their quest for God, the only "god" they know is their pastor. The only semblance of the divine they encounter is the man in a sacred robe with embroidered crosses, wearing a cross of gold around his neck, whom they hear preaching. Unless they find God, this is whom they "get."

Any safety and solace they find in this "sweet hour" of prayer is truly meaningful, especially when they have to go back into an abusive home for the remainder of the week.

But when the man leading the congregation of the devout, who represents the "Divine" to them, or is the only "god" they know, tragically lures them into a devastating encounter, in the minds of many girls and women, God Himself has done this to them. In their worldview, they finally "found" God, and found that He is no different. Yet many women and, hopefully, little girls too, have the mental ability to distinguish between the God of protection and "preying pastors." Fortunately, little Anna Mae did not run into this in her church; but her experience, nevertheless, condemned her to a life without sanctuary.

Though God's "own" rejected her, she truly became a source of cultural enrichment for the world to appreciate. She truly was God's own.

She paid a heavy price for what she became in the world, years of severe physical beatings and mental anguish, trapped. Had she found acceptance in the Church as a little girl, she might have sought refuge in the Church. However, with the door of the Church being the way to pain and rejection due to her past, she sought spiritual guidance through the only way her mind could conceive when one of her backup singers taught her another way to meditate.

Only the abused can best relate to Miss Turner's spiritual journey. We who cannot relate, we who have not walked in her shoes might be amiss to judge. It is truly quizzical that the world embraces God's gift of Miss Turner without understanding the source.

All abused women whether inside or outside of the Church are accepted by God. He offers healing and restoration to a life of sanctuary, solitude, and spirituality. He offers strength to speak out against offense and to resist and run from predators wherever they may be found—whether inside or outside the Church. It does not matter. If the Church does not listen, God has His own strategically located contingent of warriors outside organized religion who can help—people who do not have a form of godliness, but truly embrace the power thereof. God's people are everywhere. This is the meaning of the true Church, the invisible, worldwide, general Church of God. The abused can truly know God and be part of His kingdom, part of His Church.

The inner dynamics of the soul are such that healing is difficult to achieve even with the aid of the Spirit of God. It is not with the snap of a finger, the flick of a light switch, or the simple petition before God that magically makes healing occur. The marring of the tables of the mind is never erased; it is impossible for the mind to forget the violation. God did not make anyone in such a manner. He created us never to forget for the sake of self-preservation. Nor should one forget. If a child forgets that touching a hot stove will burn his finger, he would be bound to make himself vulnerable to the tragedy. Remembrance is a gift of God. The ability to teach others of the pitfalls of life is based on the innate ability to remember past experiences.

Perception of one's self plays a crucial role in victimization. People with low self-esteem have a propensity to invite invaders to victimize them to gain a false sense of acceptance and a pretentious sense of self-worth, and negative attention. This dynamic is like a whirlpool, which further mars the mind, ruining the spirit. To say this demoralizes people is a vast understatement. Sometimes the damage to one's soul is beyond repair, yet, not beyond forgiveness. However, forgiveness is required in the healing process. Yet it is not easily given, and sometimes forgiving is impossible without God's intervention.

Some victims simply lose the will to regain self-respect. Lost virtue is hard to find. Those needing motivation are truly emotionally dependent on others, and such vulnerability makes them easy prey to those who would use them.

Perpetrators' tools of deception include flattery, empty words, filling emotional needs that are actually based on selfish ambition, money, empty promises, things, intimidation, and threats.

Self-worth is a fleeting dynamic.

The community of the devout can suddenly become the community of the devil as they turn love into hatred toward victims of sexual abuse within their vestibules.

Dr. Jim Linzey

Personality Summary: Dr. Clancy McKenzie

When leaders are without accountability most can be categorized with sociopathic tendencies; there are unpredictable traits that manifest and increases the potential for them to do harm to those with whom they engage, which include multiple areas in their life being soiled by indiscretions simply because for millions, the human condition recognizes "grace" as liberty to continue. Many become "Megalomaniacs."

Simply defined:

1. A psychopathological condition characterized by delusional fantasies of wealth, power, or omnipotence.

2. An obsession with grandiose or extravagant things or actions.

In other words, if I got away this long, what and who can stop me now, and why?

When leadership goes rouge...

In general, individuals involved in multiple relationships that have lasted for extended periods of time have mastered dulling their conscience, and amplifies a spiral decline that most aren't aware is happening. This sociopathic behavior induces an ideology of invincibility, entitlement, and fuels grandiose expectations where one's perception become distorted and he or she is unable to distinguish what is a healthy reality. In both men and women.

Identifying Telltale Signs

The following are traits that are characteristic to

sociopaths. Remember that most people exhibit at least some of these personality traits to some degree. The key is to look for extreme and repetitive instances of these traits.

Consider the individual's personality and mannerisms.
Sociopaths are usually extremely charming and charismatic. Their personalities are described as magnetic, and as such, they generate a lot of attention and praise from others. They also tend to have strong sexual energy, and may have strange sexual fetishes or be sex addicts.

- *Sociopaths are great orators. They usually use poetic language and are able to carry on long monologues or stories that are hypnotic and capture the attention of those around them.*

- *Sociopaths have delusions of grandeur, and oftentimes feel overly entitled to certain positions, people, and things. They believe that their own beliefs and opinions are the absolute authority, and disregard the opinions of others.*

- *Sociopaths are rarely shy, insecure, or at a loss for words. They have trouble suppressing emotional responses like anger, impatience, or annoyance, and constantly lash out at others and respond hastily to these emotions.*

One may ask why?

Sociopaths are such dominant leaders; they are usually able to attract a following of some kind. The followers tend to be weaker, more passive individuals who have been intoxicated by the sociopath's charm.

- *Sociopaths are incapable of experiencing guilt or shame for their actions. They rarely apologize for their behavior, and while aware of the emotional, physical, and financial repercussions of their actions on others, they just don't care (and may even enjoy inflicting and witnessing such effects). As a result, they betray, threaten, and harm those around them without feeling any type of remorse.*

- Sociopaths are manipulative. They constantly try to influence and dominate the people around them, and tend to seek positions of leadership.

Life is a struggle for survival, dominance, or success, it is WAR. And once a person's mind has been stretched by experiences, it is impossible to return to being satisfied with previous norms. This is one reason why men who have never obtained any professional achievements prior to his role as pastor, finds himself thrust into a rock star arena for which he is not prepared having no previous points of reference of *splendor* and success. The entrapments are the same: *women, women, women,* and more *women,* who are willing to participate at any level, just so as they can be close to the "limelight," and part of a *special breed*.

Men who lose sight of purpose and selectively applies any moral tenets is a candidate destined to be toppled. If not totally, partially, and his effectiveness is marred and potential diminished where he serves and he often leaves a trail of distressed individuals behind. He sees himself as a god and people are merely subjects in need of a ruler.

- Sociopaths are incapable of experiencing love, and likely will not have had healthy romantic relationships in the past. They are only concerned with their own interests, and use compassion as a tool to manipulate others, but are not genuinely compassionate.

Why women follow? ...

Physically abused women who have never escaped and healed from the infected cycle of abuse find themselves (unconsciously) enslaved, and devoted to serve preachers unconditionally. Many see it as a duty, and value the opportunity to be with that man as somehow different, and special.

The preacher's wife is disdained in the eyes of these females, discarding her legal rights as immaterial and something they don't have to consider, and many don't, which has led to numerous breakdowns in ministries. With that said, it must be accentuated that most women only stay in a disruptive mode when they are encouraged by interaction with a male (it doesn't mean women won't attempt to allure a man, it simply means that if a man is very clear about his position women are less likely to intentionally cause disruption in his home).

Regardless of a female's education or standing in life, if she has never been nurtured from a child, there is a deep void to be validated. She looks for her father to grant approval even though the relationship is twisted because she too, will serve the sexual needs of a pastor hoping to gain acceptance.

Sadly, when one is not committed to build a healthy lifestyle for him or her, the individual settles for living vicariously through the lenses of others; the engagement in the temporary satisfies a void that many are not willing to address so they mask, and medicate in order to prevent facing themselves in the mirror, ALONE.

Just as with any addiction, those who find themselves entangled in these types of relationships will only be stronger enough to remove themselves when they make a decision it is enough, and seek counseling. It is imperative that you become accountable to someone, a person who will keep you honest and challenged to do the right thing. Sexual addiction isn't any different.

"CHURCH GIRLS" the Seduction of Religion

The Parallel Composition to Spiritual Decadence

Priest, pastor, prophet, preacher, exhorter, shepherd, evangelist, apostle, elder, overseer, reverend, and bishop are some of the terms used to signify the person charged with the care and feeding of God's human flock. The shepherd and sheep allusion to Psalms 23 is commonplace within the Christian tradition. What happens however, when the shepherd has sexual relations with his sheep? This controversial practice is termed bestiality and/or zoophilia. Zoophilia is the attraction of shepherds to sheep, while bestiality is the actual consummating act of intercourse between shepherd and sheep. Are zoophilia and bestiality legal? Even more, are zoophilia and bestiality biblically permitted?

What shall we say then to the prevailing practice of preachers using parishioners as sexual prey?

Oliver-Brown and Hollis in their book, <u>Church Girls: The Seduction of Religion</u>, provide us a rare glimpse into the dark underbelly of pimp preachers, sanctified seductions, and an unholy harlotry growing in several church communities. Too many congregations have pews occupied by sexually starved and spiritually malnourished women who gaze upon the exalted platform as the platter from which to select a satisfying male entrée. Conversely, many pulpits are propagated by gifted men who fail to acknowledge the spiritual and physical vacuum created by ministry, and thus find themself seeking emotional fulfillment and sexual satisfaction in the perched breasts and warm thighs of a church sister's embrace.

<u>Church Girls</u> is a must read for anyone interested in the asymmetrical power relationship between men and women in the church, as well as the call and response traditions between pulpit and pew (much less between saint and sinner).

-- Dr. M. Christopher Brown II is a clergyman, university administrator, and scholar of organizational theory, public policy, educational equity, sociology, and systematic theology. He is the author/editor of 17 books and

monographs; and has lectured and/or presented scholarship in various countries on six of seven continents – Africa, Asia, Australia, Europe, North America, and South America.

"CHURCH GIRLS" the Seduction of Religion

RESOURCE INDEX

National Association of Psychologists www.nasponline.org/

American Association of Couples and Sex Therapists
www.aacast.net

National Coalition Against Domestic Violence
www.ncadv.org

Photos: Shutterstock/ Internet public domain

National Association of Sex Therapists

Monday, January 21, 2013 Commentaries Clergy sex abuse and "the silence of the many." [Source Internet] page 17

The Parallel Composition Dr. Chris M. Brown, University Administrator

Clergy abuse is a serious offense…if you have a bonafide case of abuse and need to discuss your options, feel free to contact these resources:
Images Courtesy of the Internet

LEGAL COUNSEL

KEVON GLICKMAN, ESQ.
Kevon@kevonglickman.com [NY NJ PA]
PACIFIC LEGAL FOUNDATION http://www.pacificlegal.org/

FOR INTERVIEWS/SPEAKING ENGAGEMENTS

The Hollis Media Group
Email: Hollismediagroup@outlook.com

Proposals/Invitations must be submitted 4 weeks in advance via email.

We anticipate many will be empowered to become conduits of positive change, many will be healed emotionally and psychologically, and their spirituality enhanced to make a difference in one's sphere of influence.

The intent of this book was to address:

- *The taboos of religion and remove the barriers of silence*
- *Expose the dereliction of duty*
- *Spiritual prostitution*
- *Complacency – the cancer of faking it*
- *The torn fabric in the religious community*
- *Psychological disorders among clergy*
- *Abuse of Power; and*
- *To offer recourse to the abused*

Hollismediagroup@outlook.com /www.hollismedia.net
"We make positive strategy happen daily!"

About the AUTHORS:

Both authors, Earnestine Oliver-Brown and Janice Hollis are accomplished professional women and business owners. Each work within their respective discipline touching the lives of thousands throughout the United States and in foreign territories through educational outreach, spiritual enrichment and by augmenting employment-training services.

In addition, both were raised in the Church and understand its culture, even that which is often hidden and forbidden discussions in some denominations. Hollis is an ordained Bishop.

They both share a love for children, especially the underserved, orphans and displaced veterans.

Their love of humanity is demonstrated in this literary project to create a voice for those who lost their ability to speak, and to stand in the gap for those who have no strength to stand. And to tell the truth regardless of what public opinion may dictate. Hollis' motto, *"Every day is the right day to do the right thing."*

www.ingramcontent.com/pod-product-compliance
Lightning Source LLC
Chambersburg PA
CBHW071916290426
44110CB00013B/1381